GHOST STORIES
STORIES
of the
APPALACHIANS

GHOST STORIES
STORIES
of the
APPALACHIANS

Susan Smitten

Lone Pine Publishing International

The Distributor: Lone Pine Publishing
1808 B Street, Suite 140
Auburn, WA USA 98001

Websites: www.lonepinepublishing.com
www.ghostbooks.net

Library and Archives Canada Cataloguing in Publication

Smitten, Susan, 1961-

   Ghost stories of the Appalachians / Susan Smitten.

   ISBN 978-1-894877-20-6

   1. Ghosts--Appalachian Region. 2. Haunted places--Appalachian Region. I. Title.

GR580.S676 2009   133.109756'8   C2009-902846-8

The stories, folklore and legends in this book are based on the author's collection of sources, including individuals whose experiences have led them to believe they have encountered phenomena of some kind or another. They are meant to entertain, and neither the publisher nor the author claims these stories represent fact.

PC: 6

Dedication

To my family—husband David and daughter Naia—who are my loving support and inspiration.

And to all those who believe in the power of a good story and have shared their stories with others.

Contents

Chapter 4: Haunted Institutions

Chapter 5: More Haunted Hotels

Chapter 6: Mountainside Haunts

Acknowledgments

Gathering the information for this book took many hands to make somewhat less challenging work. I wish to thank all the contributors to this collection of stories; without them there would not be a book. In particular, I extend my thanks to those who helped at the outset when the task at hand felt just this side of overwhelming: Frankie McWhorter of the North Carolina Division of Tourism, Mary Johnson of West Virginia Archives and History, the North Carolina Office of Archives and History, and The Filson Historical Society.

Also I wish to thank the individuals and groups who went an extra mile to be of assistance: Angela Moore, Erin Connarn, Polly Gear, Joe Wright of Paranormal Scene Investigators, Tracy Franklin of the East Tennessee Paranormal Research Society, Sarah Harrison of the Asheville Paranormal Society, Andrea Jamison of Spirit Hunters of Knoxville, the Haunt Masters Club, and Peace River Ghost Trackers.

And I am grateful for the guidance and good sense of the team at Lone Pine Publishing, especially my editor, Sheila Quinlan.

Introduction

There is a logical explanation for everything—right? Doors slam because they were suddenly moved by a gust of wind through an open window. Floorboards creak as old houses shift and settle. Missing objects reappear in bizarre places because our less-than-perfect memories forgot where we stashed them. Shadows in the night are just light shaped by moving curtains.

That's the rational mind offering sensible, practical solutions to ostensibly normal situations. But then there is the prickly thought that maybe, just maybe, there is another explanation, especially when the inexplicable happens, such as a goblet floating in mid-air or a person walking through a wall. Reason makes way for another possibility: maybe it was a ghost.

Now *ghost* is a loaded word. Paranormal experts the world over debate the terms used to describe paranormal phenomena. But regardless of what you choose to call entities of the spectral realm, roughly half of the population in the United States believes in them.

There are lots of reasons why people suppose ghosts share our air space. Ghosts are trapped here by strong passions: love, hate, anger, despair. They stay to complete tasks, fulfill promises or seek vengeance. In some cases they don't realize they are dead. Some ghosts seem to relive one particular moment over and over; others manifest for a fleeting instant never to return.

In the Appalachians, where one mountaintop is as different from another as is geographically possible, the ghosts also come in many metaphoric shapes and sizes. This 200,000-square-mile region is literally too big for one book.

The spine of the Appalachian Mountains runs from southern New York through to northern Mississippi and takes in bits of every state on either side of the ridge, plus the whole of West Virginia. In this collection, I concentrated on the southern region of Appalachia, particularly Tennessee, North Carolina, Virginia and West Virginia. Perhaps a sequel is in order.

I agree with historian Patty A. Wilson, who says, "A region's ghost stories represent the history of a people and reflect their culture, beliefs and hopes." The people interviewed for these stories reflect a diverse and diverting culture, steeped in gracious hospitality and yet still connected to rugged pioneering roots. Another amazing thing—astounding to me—was the longevity of the family lines in one place. I met so many people who live in the home of their great-great-great-*great*-grandparent. On top of that, one ghost story often led to another. It seems nearly everyone in the Appalachians has seen or heard tell of a ghost or three.

So, with that, I offer this collection of stories—some are amusing, some are frightening and some are thought-provoking; all are meant to entertain. Many of the older, some might even say obvious, ghost stories of the Appalachians, such as the Mothman of West Virginia, are not included here. In gathering these stories, I tended to favor places that have current experiences to share. Many of the stories in this book have never been told before, and some of the legends have been told so many times, in both book and film, that I didn't feel I could add much that was new. I hope you enjoy exploring the unusual tales of spirits and specters of the Appalachians.

1
Haunted
Homes

The Green River Plantation

Rutherfordton, North Carolina

How would you feel about living in a place where ghosts come to visit on the first of each month? Ellen Cantrell owns the Green River Plantation, a lovely mansion tucked away in the hills of western North Carolina, and she says her historic home may belong to her on paper, but she shares it with spirits from times past. "I've always felt somebody here," says Ellen in her soft southern accent. "I rarely feel afraid if I'm alone. When I go from space to space in the house, it feels as though someone is with me."

There are clues to substantiate Ellen's feelings. At the start of each month one particular door in the house opens, as if the unseen presence walks in to announce it has arrived. Sometimes Ellen catches something moving out of the corner of her eye as if something just walked by. In addition, she periodically picks up the smell of cologne wafting through the house, but it is not a fragrance she or anyone in her family wears. "It isn't like the fragrances of today," she says.

Ellen also says they often hear things "that just don't make sense." For example, one night she awoke to the sound of a child calling out to her. She had started to get up when her husband reminded her that the child they have guardianship of was not home that evening. "The next morning," recalls Ellen, "my daughter came down and said, 'You have to do something about the crying out because it woke me up twice last night.' She was shocked when I told her there was no one here."

Two men who at separate times rented the Cantrells' downstairs apartment said they heard someone walking upstairs when no one was there. One of the men was Ellen's brother. "He wanted his girlfriend to come over because he said the sound was driving him crazy, and she told him *he* was crazy if he thought she would come over."

The plantation, with its stately four-story mansion and 356 acres of lush land, overlooks the floodplain of the Green River. Joseph McDowell Carson built the oldest sections of the home between 1804 and 1807. The plantation stayed within the Carson family for six generations before being sold in 1958. After that it passed from owner to owner, eventually sitting uninhabited for five years until the Cantrells purchased it in 1987. By then the plantation had seen better days. The luster of its former glory had faded with neglect, and it fell to Eugene and Ellen Cantrell to roll up their sleeves and enthusiastically take on restoration of the great home. No detail was too small, right down to recreating original paint colors and floor finishes.

The project was a labor of love for Ellen, whose grandfather confided in her when she was only 10 years old that he would have loved to own the plantation. She feels that she honored her grandfather's dream by restoring the mansion. Now, as the plantation celebrates its bicentennial, Ellen and her daughter Amanda host tours by reservation though the historic site and allow people to rent various spaces, including the gorgeous boxwood gardens and lawns, for special events. As a venue, the Green River Plantation is quite popular with both the living and the dearly departed.

Rather than leave it to their imaginations or speculation, the Cantrells took action to investigate the ghosts in their home. They invited a team from Forest City—Paranormal Scene Investigators—to hunt for proof that there are supernatural phenomena on the premises.

Joe Wright, founder and team leader of PSI, conducted two investigations. Joe's philosophy is to eliminate all possible human causes before classifying anything as paranormal. His group goes to great lengths, using digital cameras, digital audio recording devices, heat sensors, compasses, even video mapping systems using flat plane lasers, to determine whether an unseen energy presence is there or not. "You'd be surprised how many people want to fool you," he told me.

But Joe takes his job seriously. He does not try to interpret the spirits he encounters; he wants only to confirm that there is unexplained energy present. "To the question what makes a ghost, I say matter and energy," he explains. If PSI cannot find any other explanation for spikes on their energy monitors, then they classify the readings as paranormal. "Paranormal meaning 'above what is normal.'"

At the Green River Plantation, the PSI team focused its investigation on the original part of the house and found plenty of energy to confirm that something or someone is trying to get the Cantrells' attention. While the team members investigated, some of them had unusual encounters.

One place where the Cantrells have experienced a lot of activity is up in the attic. Apparently in the late 1800s or early 1900s, a mentally challenged girl named Rebecca lived there. "We don't know why they kept her locked up there, but she wasn't right," says Ellen. "We don't know if she had bipolar disorder or what. I haven't seen anything, but others claim to have seen a small girl with a white gown on."

On one occasion, Ellen's daughter Amanda had a friend visiting with a three-year-old daughter. They left the daughter sleeping in Amanda's apartment with a baby monitor nearby and were surprised to hear the little girl saying, "Leave me alone. Get away from me!" Amanda and her friend rushed to check on the girl, who told them, "Get that little girl away from me. I don't want her here."

Many people who go up to the attic experience being touched. A friend of the Cantrells told the PSI team that she is overcome with sadness whenever she is up there, and she also gets a tingling sensation, almost a full-body chill.

Despite that advance knowledge, PSI team member Todd Kiser was completely surprised when he felt an odd sensation, as if a child was taking his hand. Joe Wright says Todd also had a flashlight in his pocket with the cord hanging out, and it was pulled. "In that second he became flustered, overwhelmed with emotion," recalls Joe. "He tried to speak but couldn't." Todd handed off his video camera and asked one of the other team members to "flash him," meaning to take a picture of him in case they could capture something digitally. Todd bent over with his hands on his knees and took some deep breaths before telling the group that he had felt as if something was draining his energy. "I'm just getting cold chills," says the visibly shaken man on the tape recorded by another PSI investigator.

During the investigation, Joe's team captured a lot of electronic voice phenomena (EVPs)—sounds that could not be heard at the time but were audible when they played the recordings back. In the attic, they caught different voices. At one point when some of the team members were talking, a recorded voice says, "We were waiting..." And to the question "Rebecca, are you up here?" a voice responds "Yes."

Another audio recording taken while out walking on the grounds behind the house picked up the sound of a woman sobbing. Ellen Cantrell says the sound makes sense because the little girl died at age nine while getting a horseback riding lesson from her father. "She was thrown from the horse."

Ellen Cantrell no longer lives in the main house—she and Eugene moved out in 2008. But tragically, her husband of 49 years died in an unexpected accident in January 2009. Ellen's beloved Eugene joins the list of spirits who protect her at the Green River Plantation. "I still put out his coffee cup in the morning."

Mary, the Ghost of Main Street

Jonesborough, Tennessee

While I was researching the other ghosts in this very haunted town, Jonesborough historian Deborah Montanti piqued my interest in a small, privately owned home on Main Street. "I know the woman who lives there, and she is adamant that she has a ghost in her house. She knows the ghost's name and has a relationship with it." I followed up with Sue Henley, the owner of this unusually haunted house, and this is her story about Mary.

Sue Henley was born not 10 minutes from Jonesborough and has lived in the area her entire life. She and her husband

Gerald bought the little home on Main Street over 20 years ago from an elderly woman who Sue refers to as Miss Martha.

The Henleys' previous house sold more quickly than expected, and they found themselves having to move into the Main Street home before it was fully renovated. Perhaps the ghost didn't like the idea of new owners, but the couple experienced an inauspicious start to their lives under their new roof. "The incidents started almost the minute we moved in. Our very first night in the house, I got locked in the bedroom. My husband Gerald used a screwdriver to get the door open. After that, we tried a hundred times to get that door to lock by itself, and it wouldn't," declares Sue.

That was just the beginning of the strange things that Sue and Gerald would come home to each day. "I worked in town, and before leaving I would turn off the radio. It was the kind that you have to turn the knob to turn off, and it would make a popping noise as it shut off. But I would come home and the radio would be blaring."

Several times the bathroom faucet somehow turned itself on, even after a concerted effort to twist it tightly shut. "My husband would come in and say, 'How many times do I have to tell you to turn off the tap?' Just five minutes earlier I would have been in there closing it, but the water was running again."

Things in the house were constantly being moved to the point of driving Sue crazy. One might think that this type of thing is easy enough to explain as absent-mindedness or her husband's misplacement of items, but Sue says that it escalated. "I have a lot of antique bowls and ornaments, and they are all on shelves. I would come home from work, and in the kitchen, half a dozen of my antiques would be sitting on the floor—not broken—just sitting there. And one day a dried rose was lying on the seat where I usually sit."

In addition, Sue often returned home to find potpourri scattered on the foyer floor and up the steps to the second floor. Concerned by the ongoing supernatural commotion, she contacted the former owner. "I asked Miss Martha, 'Are there any ghosts in your house?' She gave me a funny look, paused and finally said, 'Well, they've never bothered me.' She lived there for 90 years."

It soon became clear that one of the two bedrooms on the upper floor belonged to the spirit in the house. "I had a friend visiting and she hadn't been here that long. She checked out the upstairs rooms and when she came back down said, 'You're going to think I'm crazy, but there's a young woman sitting on the floor in one bedroom by the fireplace with her knees drawn up to her chest." Sue laughs because now when people come downstairs after touring the second floor, she knows the first words out of their mouth will probably be, "You're going to think I'm crazy…"

"My niece didn't want to stay in there at first," recalls Sue. "Finally she worked up the courage. On her first night sleeping in the room, she heard someone walk in. She told me the next day that she didn't open her eyes because she was afraid to look. Something sat down on the bed, and then she felt a heavy weight on her body. It only lasted a few seconds and then lifted. My niece said after that she felt she had made peace with the ghost and was not afraid of it anymore."

The same thing happened soon after to another guest in the room. A woman who runs the nearby ice cream parlor stayed overnight, and the next day at breakfast told Sue she had tried to scream but could not get a sound out. The heavy weight pinning her to the bed lifted as suddenly as it had occurred.

It took some time before Sue had a name for her resident spirit. "I called her Mary because years and years ago, one night when I could not sleep for my husband's snoring, I came down to sleep on the sofa and had a dream that I was driving home. I was crossing the River Bridge, and when I looked over, there was a woman sitting in the passenger seat. She said, 'My name is Mary, and I want to tell you why I'm in your house.' She went on to explain that it was the last place she and her husband were happy before the Civil War. I recall that she had on a long skirt, a beige blouse and her hair was pulled back, but I don't recall her face."

After more than two decades of sharing her home with Mary, Sue describes the ghost as "a mischievous little thing." As an example, one Christmas Day while fixing dinner Sue had the table set and was standing in the family room talking to her husband and mother-in-law. Something caught her eye in the dining room, so she turned and saw that all her cutlery had been crossed. "Now I can imagine one set being crossed, but *all* of them?"

Mischief now and then turns to malice. One year while decorating for Christmas, Sue put a Madonna that had a glass globe over it and candles on a dresser in Mary's room. The next day Sue went into the bedroom to discover that the whole thing had been thrown onto floor and smashed. "I just said, 'Well we know one thing—she's not Catholic.'" That incident turned the tide for Sue's husband and made a believer of him.

The only other destructive moment caught Sue by surprise. "I was washing dishes one night when an antique toothpick holder flew off the shelf, soared straight across the room and hit the hearth, breaking into a zillion pieces."

For the next couple of years things quieted down, and Sue thought perhaps Mary had left. But it seems the spirit was just dozing. A visiting paranormal investigator actually saw Mary and described the same clothing that Sue saw in her dream. The next day when Sue awoke, she opened her bedroom door and on the floor lay an antique postcard. "I don't know *where* that card came from, but written around the edges it said, 'I thought I had better write to let you know I am not dead.' That gave me a start!"

Unlike so many of Sue's houseguests, she has never seen Mary, nor does she want to. The Henleys do not plan to move though, so they will just continue their very interesting cohabitation of the historic home on Main Street. And please, should you be visiting Jonesborough, do remember that this is a private residence, and be respectful.

The Beleaguered Betts Farm

Grantsville, West Virginia

Farmer Collins Betts likely would have died in obscurity in Calhoun County, West Virginia, if it wasn't for the fact that he lived in the most haunted house that area has ever seen. And you don't have to take his word for the house's reputation; dozens of reputable people from ministers to army captains stayed in the most haunted room of the house near

Grantsville, and all of them left wishing they had traveled on a little farther before settling in for the night.

Headless ghosts, a predatory incubus and bedding torn off by unseen hands—those top the list of horrible visitations and strange happenings within the walls of the rather unremarkable farmhouse. It is all captured in a detailed article written by a determined reporter from the *Cincinnati Enquirer* in March 1886, some 20 years after news of the hauntings circulated throughout the county. Now, nearly 125 years later, the people of Grantsville still cite the Betts incidents as among the most startling and frankly hard to explain in the county's history.

The Betts' one-story homestead sprawled along the bank of the Little Kanawha River about three miles outside of town. Until it earned a reputation for being haunted, it was well placed as a stop for travelers. But the death of a wayfaring peddler put a stop to that. The peddler disappeared after leaving Grantsville with $1000 in his pocket. His body was found not far from the Betts farm in a makeshift grave, but Collins Betts told police he had never seen the man and was never considered a suspect in the murder. Innocent or not, his house went from peaceful to plagued by the paranormal almost overnight. Actually, no one could ever say for sure that the peddler's demise had a direct connection to the onset of supernatural trouble for the Betts family, but the two events did happen about the same time.

The family began hearing inexplicable noises, such as water dripping into tin pans when neither rain nor pan was in sight. The women in the house reported hearing the creepy sound of whispering and the disturbing thump of a body hitting the floor in one of the rooms. In the chill of the night, bedding was somehow yanked off the sleeping family members. A person could get used to such things, but that was just the start. One bedroom in particular became the center for a nasty spirit. And enough people stayed in the room—why, one might reasonably wonder—to have a litany of documented eerie experiences.

Methodist minister Rev. Wayne Kennedy has the dubious honor of being the first overnight guest who got more than he bargained for. He stopped in while traveling through West Virginia and agreed to sleep in the room. Some time shortly after midnight, the minister awoke feeling as if he was being smothered. As he came more fully to his senses, he saw a shape that resembled a large black dog sitting on his chest, preventing him from moving and restricting his breath. The *Cincinnati Enquirer* reported that "it was with the greatest difficulty that he was enabled to throw off the incubus and release himself from the deadly pressure." The most common definition of an incubus is a male demon believed to lie on sleeping people and to have sexual intercourse with sleeping women. And it often takes the form of a large, black dog.

Rev. Kennedy barely waited for sunrise before packing up and leaving, swearing as he left that he would never spend another night at the Betts farmhouse. So when word of his horrifying experience got around, it would make sense that other people would stay away. Curiosity and bravado, however, kept the guests coming.

Collins' brother John could not resist the challenge of debunking the stories. He traveled from his home in Colorado to laugh at his brother's fearful countenance and ridicule the rumors of phantoms in the bedroom. John had no time for people who believed in ghosts. So the strapping, muscular man closed the door on his family and prepared to take on the phantom. Apparently, the phantom won.

The next morning, Collins went to check on his brother when he did not appear and found him lying in his bed unable to move. The helpless man told Collins that sometime in the night he felt himself being crushed under the weight of an unseen presence, and he could not shake it off. John "suffered torment until daylight, when the oppression ceased, but he had lost the use of his limbs." He left a broken man who never recovered full use of his arms and legs.

Others who stayed in the room did not suffer to the same extent—maybe they didn't go in with the same arrogance—but they still suffered. Captain Hayhurst woke to the sight of a headless man standing by his bed. Timber baron Henry Newman had his bedding ripped off no less than three times. Both men left saying they would never return.

Whatever started haunting the Betts home did not let a few walls trap it into being a homebody. Stories of strange events came back from people traveling near the farm. James Wolverton and his son heard what sounded like the cavalry galloping toward them as they drove their oxcart home one evening. As the sounds of hooves pummeling the ground and sabers rattling in scabbards drew near, the father and son got to the top of the hill and were stunned to see no one else on the road below them. But the roar of the horses grew so loud that Wolverton cried out, "My God, men, don't ride over me!" To his astonishment, the phantom troop ceased its charge. Wolverton and his son swore that it happened until their dying days.

One of Collins Betts' nephews rode past the farm on his way home, and as he and his horse got about halfway up the hill opposite the house, there was a strange apparition that spooked the horse, causing it to throw its rider and run away. The horse refused to come out of the woods until the next day, when it was coaxed back out onto the road.

What could have caused such paranormal mayhem? Maybe a natural hallucinogen? According to the *Cincinnati Enquirer*, some people put forth the theory that the farm sat on some sort of underground bed of gas, "which arises from the earth and is inhaled."

But the Betts ghosts refuse to be explained away so simply. An earlier article in the *Enquirer*, from September 30, 1884, said, "There is no doubt that Calhoun County has a mystery which neither time, bullets, courage nor philosophy can either drive away or explain. It has come to stay. If you meet a Calhouner just mention it, and he will tell you that the 'Betts ghost' is a county possession which it will gladly dispose of at any price."

Bells from Beyond

Tryon, North Carolina

In a quaint historic home in downtown Tryon, North Carolina, in the foothills of the lush Blue Ridge Mountains, Melinda Leake lives with her family—including her dear and departed great-grandmother. The spirit of her family matriarch, it would appear, likes to keep an eye on the next generations.

Melinda is no stranger to the paranormal. She works at the Foothills Equestrian Nature Center (FENCE), which is about six minutes from her home, and details of her experiences there can be found on page 120 in this book. In both places, Melinda was surprised by the presence of an otherworldly energy, though, she says, "I don't let things like that bother me." But unlike at work, at home her encounters with the spirit world have a distinctly personal feel.

The house was built in the late 1800s, a time when Tryon was just developing as a resort town where tourists could come to enjoy the mountain views and hospitable climate. The building is listed as one of the oldest homes that is still inhabited. It was among the first to be built with central heating, "so we have chimneys with no fireplaces." It belonged to Melinda's great-grandmother, who lived in the house until her death in 1987.

Melinda's mother had moved in toward the end to help care for her ailing grandmother. "She [Melinda's great-grandmother] lived in the basement suite and we lived upstairs. I was only four at the time," recalls Melinda. "She had a bell that she would ring if she needed anything, like help to go to the bathroom or something to drink."

Two days after Melinda's great-grandmother died, the first unusual incident occurred while the house slept. "Her bell started ringing," says Melinda, "but it was loud, as if she was standing in the same room looking over us. My mom and I both woke up. My mom was half-asleep and said to me, 'Okay, I'll go get her.' And then we realized, *wait* a minute..." Melinda says what struck her about the event is that both she and her mother were awakened by the sound.

On another occasion, Melinda and her mother found themselves locked out of their bedrooms. "The doors have skeleton keys, but we painted over the keyholes a long time ago. We never used the keys to lock them," she says. It was quite late, and Melinda and her mother headed upstairs to get ready for bed. They were stunned to find both bedroom doors closed, and no matter how much they pushed, the doors remained stubbornly shut. "Mom looked at me and I looked at her," Melinda says, "and Mom asked me if I had a key. I said no. So then I banged on the door and jokingly said out loud, 'Come on, Nana! It's 12:30, we're tired and we want to go to bed. No more joking around!' And then the doors opened right up."

The presence of a family spirit provides Melinda with some comfort. "I'm raising my children there now." When her oldest son was a baby, he particularly enjoyed sitting in a swing with a timer on it. He was only a few months old, just able to raise his head, and Melinda noticed that he always focused his attention on a place just to his right. "He would look and laugh for hours. We always joked that it was his guardian angel. He would be laughing out loud and jiggling as if someone was tickling him," she recalls. "He did that for several months, and even though he couldn't talk, it was as though he was carrying on a conversation with some unseen person sitting next to him."

Perhaps her son's personal playmate can be explained away as a child's innately imaginative spirit, but there is another concrete example of having a ghost in the house. In the kitchen, Melinda recently witnessed a coffee cup travel along the counter from one end to the other—by itself. "I looked to see if there was water on the counter that might account for it moving, and there wasn't. But even if there had been, it would have needed a push to get it started."

So it seems that her great-grandma still has a way of letting her family know that she continues to watch over them...and their dirty dishes. Melinda isn't bothered, and she would be thrilled if her great-grandma felt like tackling the laundry!

Angela's Story

Marion, North Carolina

Born and raised in the foothills of western North Carolina, Angela Moore is a self-taught psychic who knew at an early age that she had a gift for sensing other energies. "I think maybe it's the nature of my being," says Angela. "I stir things up."

Even so, the woman couldn't quite believe her eyes when she arrived home one night with her family to see a doll staring out the living room window as if it was searching the street for her wayward caregivers. Although the experience happened nearly 20 years ago, she remembers it clearly. "That house was weird. It was a little, itty bitty square house, not fancy, but it was creepy. And a lot of things happened there."

Among the eerie things was a little toy car that flew across the room by itself and a shirt that disappeared and reappeared. Angela remembers the day the matchbox car moved on its own. "I was standing at the stove and my husband was sweeping out the carport. I heard a little car come from the door and go bouncing across the room. I thought my husband had tossed it in, but when I leaned back to tell him dinner was ready I saw the door was shut. And it also dawned on me that he was sweeping on the other side of the carport," she says. "But I saw that car go flying."

On another occasion, Angela and her husband were preparing to go out for the night. Her husband was getting dressed, and he hung his shirt on the doorknob. But when he went to put it on, the shirt wasn't there. "He looked behind the door, on the floor, even under the bed," says Angela. "We both looked all over for it. Then we looked up and it was on the doorknob." She pauses, then says with emphasis: "I'm telling you it was *not* there. There were two of us, not one of us having a mental breakdown."

But the event that sent shivers through Angela occurred as they arrived home from a night of Christmas celebrations. She included it in her book *Through Angela's Eyes* because of the lasting impact it had on her. Angela, her husband and their two children drove up to the house, still reveling in a happy holiday and planning for the year ahead when they noticed a figure in the window. Angela could plainly see a doll with its plastic face pressed to the window and its little hands cupped up to its head as if peering into the darkness. The window glowed with a yellow light. "It was *very* weird," says Angela. She and her husband joked that it reminded them of an episode of *The Twilight Zone*.

As she got the kids out of the car, Angela thought that it must be an odd coincidence. She assumed her daughter had left the doll propped on the back of the sofa and that it had either fallen against the window or her daughter had posed it before they left. Then she remembered: there was no sofa under the window; they had moved it to make room for the Christmas tree and had not yet moved it back. As she processed that disturbing thought, her husband pointed out that they had turned all the lights off when they left—where was the light was coming from?

Now feeling more anxious than amused, they went inside the house. More surprises awaited them. The house was dark; there were no lights on. And when they turned on the living room light, the doll was sitting in a chair on the other side of the room. "I now think that it wasn't a ghost at all," muses Angela. "Instead I feel it was a mischievous otherworldly entity."

They moved soon after because the house was making everyone feel afraid. And as odd as it may seem, Angela is grateful for the weirdness. It was that house, and particularly the doll in the window, that got her to thinking that perhaps she might have an extraordinary ability to tune into the paranormal. "I didn't realize then that I was psychic, but I also thought, it's not possible that every place I live can be haunted."

But even after years of connecting to the spirits of those who once lived in the area, she says it still freaks her out when she actually sees them—especially when they are sitting on her front porch.

Some years ago, Angela returned home for an appointment with one of her clients. As she pulled up in her car, she could see her client waiting for her on the front porch. "As I looked harder to see who it was, I realized there were two women on the front porch, my client and another woman who stood up as I arrived," says Angela. "She was tall and very thin, had long, dark, almost stringy hair, and wore a sundress. She looked like someone I went to church with, but I didn't know her. I continued to look hard at her because I was trying to remember where I knew her from."

Angela got out of her car and walked up the steps to the gate that keeps her dogs inside. She could still see the two women waiting for her. She bent down to unlatch the gate, and when she looked up again, only one woman stood on the front porch. "I said to my client, 'Where did she go?' The woman said, 'Who?' And I said, 'The woman behind you!' She said, 'There is no one. I'm the only one here.' After all these years you'd think I'd be used to it," Angela tells me, "but it still shocks me."

A few days later, another woman came to see Angela for a session. Angela answered the door and was surprised to see that her client had a child with her. "A little girl about seven years old stood behind her, and she was kind of hanging onto the woman's dress," she recalls. "She had long, dark, stringy hair and really big eyes. And I distinctly remember she was wearing a tube top. What struck me is that the woman looked upper middle class and the kid looked poor." Without judging, Angela remembers thinking that the two didn't seem to fit. As well, the woman was very poised and sure of herself while the little girl seemed shy.

Angela stepped back so that the woman could walk in, and no child followed. She looked out the door, but there was no one there. "I asked the woman about it. She gave me a strange look and said she had come alone. Then it occurred to me that the girl looked like a child version of the woman I had seen on the porch a few days ago.

"The story continues," Angela tells me, laughing. "It does go somewhere." Later on that night Angela and her husband had the front door open because of the heat, and while sitting in living room, they heard a woman's voice call from the dark, "Angie, can I come on in?" The voice sounded like a friend of Angela's, but something kept Angela from responding. "There was no car, it's dark, and we didn't hear anyone come up the steps. So I didn't move. It was weird, but I had a sense that I should *not* be answering. My husband, meanwhile, ran straight to the door to tell her to come in. He could see out, and there was nobody there." Angela felt her instinct to stay silent had been confirmed. "Somebody wanted in, and she needed me to invite her. But you have to be careful what you invite into your home. Not all spirits are created equal."

As she pondered the incidents, from seeing the woman and the child to hearing the voice call her name, Angela kept getting one strong impression in her mind. "I kept thinking of this spirit and getting an image of the huge old tree out on the front of my property. I know that seems strange, but no matter how I tried to think of it, I would see that big ol' tree."

A few days after hearing the disembodied voice, Angela arrived home to see another woman sitting on the porch, waiting for a session with her. The woman couldn't wait for Angela to arrive and was practically bursting at the seams to share something with her. "I'm going to tell you something, but you'll think I'm crazy," she said to Angela. "While sitting here looking at that oak tree, I kept thinking I saw a woman in the tree. She was skinny with long, dark hair."

Angela now feels sure that someone's spirit is caught in the oak tree, but she isn't sure what to do about it. "I have never experienced anything like this," she says. "Regardless, I still feel there is something attached to that oak tree. Maybe a spirit from long ago was buried there and the tree took root around it. I don't know. But sitting on the porch in the shade has definitely taken on a new feeling."

The Phantom at Pine Hill

Martinsburg, West Virginia

Growing up in the Appalachians, surrounded by whispering hills and well-known "haints," Don Wood knows about ghosts. As the president of the Berkeley County Historical Society, he is one of the keepers of history for the second oldest county in West Virginia, and knowing the history means knowing the ghosts. The area is infamous for the Wizard Clip (see next page) and Harper's Ferry ghosts.

Some of the stories are closer to home—Don's mother's home, to be exact. "My mother used to talk about the spooky, haunted house on a farm in what is called the Pine Hill, south of Martinsburg, near the Douglas Grove area." Martinsburg sits along the old Cumberland Trail, which was a major route during the 1700s and 1800s for people traveling to all points west. But this particular ghost decided to stay put.

Don's grandmother bought the farm in 1917 from a man named Benjamin Cook. There were two houses on the property. According to Don's mother, the family moved into the newer, better house of the two and lived there for three years. But over those years, it became clear that the deed to the land had come with an unexpected extra. Something spectral regularly gave the family a reason to think that they were not the only ones living there.

"My mother said that at night you would hear a carriage drive up to the house and stop, but when you looked there was no one there," Don wrote in an article for a local newspaper. "When you were upstairs at night, you could be awakened by someone sawing meat on the kitchen table. Someone would walk up the stairs and stop at the top stair." The family would also watch as doors to the house opened when no one was there.

Finally having had enough, Don's grandmother sold the property. But the new title-holder of the farm was to discover something even more shocking. When he came home one day, the owner "found a dead man sitting in a chair with his whiskey bottle by him." He promptly tore the house down and moved into the older tenant house.

Interestingly, Don's grandmother did not leave the ghosts of Berkeley County behind by moving. She relocated to Opequon Creek near the Tabler Mill place. "You could not go near the hollow along the creek after dark," says Don. "A headless woman would appear."

The Wizard Clip

Middleway, West Virginia

For many people growing up in Berkeley County, West Virginia, some of the first stories their parents shared were tales of haunting and witchcraft. Stories were handed down from mothers to daughters, who often studied magic and believed whole-heartedly in the power of witches.

Few tales compare to the Wizard Clip—one of the strangest and, oddly enough, one of the best documented. Perhaps it is not surprising that a lot of ink has been dedicated to keeping this story alive in the Appalachians. After all, it has the makings of a blockbuster movie: a strange visitor who dies suddenly, a poltergeist with a penchant for cutting things to ribbons, ghostly horses galloping through the night, mysterious livestock deaths, barns burning... And to think it all took place at the end of the 18th century. An article in the *Shepherdstown Register* on November 9, 1922, quoted Rev. Alfred E. Smith, editor-in-chief of the *Baltimore Catholic Review*, as saying that the tale of the bizarre incidents on the land once owned by a farmer named Adam Livingston "is the truest ghost story ever told."

The Livingstons were a hard-working farm family from Pennsylvania who moved to the eastern tip of West Virginia with their three boys and four girls to work their 70 acres of land and make the best life they could. The year was 1794: George Washington was still president, Eli Whitney got a patent to the cotton gin, the French Revolution was in full swing and the turn of the century neared.

According to several accounts, a stranger appeared on the farmer's doorstep and asked if he might stay. Some versions indicate the man was already ill; others suggest he lived at the farm as a boarder and became sick. Either way the ending is the same: the man's illness worsened to the point where he asked for a priest to be brought to administer last rites. Livingston refused. It turns out Livingston held tight to his Lutheran beliefs—some say he was intensely bigoted—and told the dying man that even if he knew where to find a priest, he would never allow one access to his home. The stranger died, nameless and without a Catholic blessing, and Livingston buried him in non-consecrated ground at the edge of the farm. Apparently that situation did not sit too well with the spirit of the dead stranger.

Overnight the peace of life on the Livingston acreage was shattered. Livingston's world became a living nightmare. Almost from the minute the man's lifeless body was covered with dirt, strange phenomena plagued the farmer and his family. It started with the sound of horses galloping in circles around the house throughout the night. Livingston peered out on the moonlit yard, but there were no animals to be seen.

There is a long list of horrible events that are said to have transpired in the days and weeks that followed. Dishes flew off the shelves and broke. Chickens literally walked around with their heads cut off, butchered by some unseen hand. The barn burned down, cows died of unknown maladies, money vanished and sourceless screams echoed through the farm buildings. The family felt terrorized but had no idea what was causing the phenomena and were powerless to stop it.

Then the clipping that gives this story its name commenced. The unseen phantom put cinema's Edward Scissorhands to shame. From dawn to dusk, the sinister sound of metal shears clicked in the house and around the farm, cutting everything in sight. Clothes, sheets, leather boots, saddles—anything malleable—were cut in an unusual spiral shape so they could not be repaired. Half-moon crescents were cut into garments while people were wearing them! The non-stop click-click-click went on for months. The predicament soon became the talk of Berkeley County, and people came from all over to witness the "Wizard Clip" for themselves. Most visitors arrived expecting a hoax and left having witnessed a haunting.

One tale that has been handed down involves the visit of a woman who took pains to protect her good silk bonnet (some report it as a shawl) from the spectral snippers. She carefully tucked the hat inside a handkerchief and hid it in her pocket. But when she left the farm and pulled out her hat, it was cut into ribbons.

Naturally every huckster and charlatan with a widget up his sleeve used this situation as an opportunity to make a buck. But no one could rid the farm of the problem. Not even the local Lutheran pastor could prevent the relentless clipping. Adam Livingston stubbornly refused to listen to his neighbors' advice and seek the help of Catholic clergy—until, that is, he had the dream.

Livingston dreamed he was struggling up a steep hill, and when he finally made it to the top he met a man in religious robes. It was not the long-bearded wise man of lore, but a cleric who told Livingston he could help him. Desperate to find his "dream man," Livingston implored some friends to help track the Catholic priest down. Livingston finally found Father Dennis Cahill presiding over a mass in Shepherdstown. As soon as Livingston saw the priest, he recognized him as the man on the mountain. He begged Father Cahill to help end his family's misery. Although reluctant, the minister visited the Livingston farm and sprinkled holy water throughout the house while praying.

Now this seems hard to believe, but in every account the story goes that as Father Cahill prepared to leave, a bag of money that had disappeared suddenly reappeared in the air and fell to the floor in the doorway. It was a good omen. For many days, the various disruptions ceased. Peace and quiet once again became the norm. The respite was short lived.

The brief rest gave renewed vigor to the phantom's penchant for slashing. Livingston appealed to Father Cahill to return. Now here the story has a few variations. Some books and a newspaper article from the *Washington Star* dated October 31, 1978, indicate that a second priest named Dimitri Gallitzen arrived at the behest of the bishop in Baltimore to investigate the story, and after three months recommended that an exorcism be performed. However, according to the *West Virginia Historical Magazine Quarterly* of January 1904, the hauntings ended when Father Cahill returned to the house to celebrate mass for the repose of the stranger's spirit. Either way, the worst of the nightmare ended for Adam Livingston and his family.

But the story does not end there. After the Wizard Clip came the Voice.

Livingston and his family converted to Catholicism, perhaps as a wave of the white flag or maybe out of gratitude. In any event, reports of a mysterious voice that guided the newly converted in how to be good Catholics soon emerged on the farm. The Voice instructed the family on religious rites such as the rosary and how to properly make a sign of the cross in the air. The disembodied religious instructor also told the family of the death of relatives who lived far away. The Voice may have even prophesied the future, for it is recorded as telling the Livingstons that their farm "will be a great place of prayer and fasting and praise."

Adam Livingston deeded 34 acres of his land to the Catholic Church. And in 1978, that land became the Priest Field Pastoral Center—a place of meditation, prayer and solitude.

In speaking to an employee currently working at the center, I was informed that there have been no incidents to report of strange occurrences. One ghost hunter reports that in the late 1990s there were some tourists who claimed to have purses, clothes and camera straps cut by something, but there is no proof of that happening. The Voice is silent. The clippers are sheathed. And one of the strangest poltergeist stories in all the Appalachians is now just that—a story.

2
Haunted Hotels

The 1889 WhiteGate Inn & Cottage

Asheville, North Carolina

She's known affectionately as Mrs. B to the current owners and guests of the 1889 WhiteGate Inn & Cottage, an elegant bed and breakfast in downtown Asheville, North Carolina. This nurturing ghost of a bygone era still walks the halls of her former convalescent home, turning off lights, closing doors and ensuring that everyone is tucked in for a peaceful night's sleep.

"For me, it is very real," says owner Frank Salvo, referring to the presence of ghosts in the house. He and Ralph Coffey bought the WhiteGate Inn in 1999 and set about turning the bed and breakfast into an oasis for travelers. Their landscaped gardens are a botanist's dream, with hundreds of varieties of rare plants, a koi pond and Ralph's prized greenhouse filled to overflowing with more than 1500 orchids and tropical plants. Indoors, the pair created a sense of relaxed luxury that starts each day with a three-course candlelit breakfast. Perhaps it is their commitment to comfort that enticed the former owner to stay on, but whatever the reason, Frank and Ralph run a spirited inn.

The previous owners briefly mentioned that there might be more to the WhiteGate property than one might list on a realtor's sale sheet. It didn't take long for Frank to tune in to the presence of more than one spirit. "Initially I was running the inn by myself, and in the early days we didn't have a lot of business so a lot of nights the rooms would be empty," explains Frank. "But I would hear footsteps, doors closing and the push-button lights going on and off. I couldn't grasp what was going on at first. And in other parts of the house, I felt sure I was being watched."

A lot of energy runs through the central hallway, and it was there that Frank had a physical encounter with one of the inn's entities. "I felt hands rubbing my shoulders, and it felt so good. I turned around to thank Ralph for the lovely massage, but there was no one there." On another occasion, as Frank was closing up the inn for the evening he heard a female voice say, "I'm right here."

What concerned Frank is that he felt distinctly uncomfortable in certain parts of the house, whereas other areas had a more soothing feel. "I knew we had more than one entity because of the different sensations."

For Ralph, the eerie, unnerving feelings were strongest in the basement storage room area. "I would walk down the stairs, and my stomach would get nauseous and my eyes would tear up," he says. He forced himself to descend the stairs because that's where they kept the canned goods and extra refrigerators, but it was never a pleasant experience.

The main house held a calm energy, but on the third floor Frank felt something constantly watching him, "and not in a good way." The range and intensity of the sensations prompted Frank to call in a local paranormal investigative team. To allow for a blind study he did not share his experiences with the team, and he was pleased when their findings of extreme energy in certain spots in the house corroborated his own encounters. "They recorded lots of whispers, the clicking sound of lights being turned on and off and identified some energy hot spots," says Frank. "That's how our documentation was started."

Soon after, a paranormal team from Duke University arrived with five students to investigate the inn. It too was a blind study, and the students included both skeptics and sensitives. They walked around the inn without any knowledge of the history of the building and later looked at 10 photographs of different people. When asked if any of the people in the pictures could be connected to the energy felt in the house, four of the five students pointed to the former owner, Mrs. Marian Bridgette—Mrs. B.

The house dates back to 1889, when it was built as a private residence. In 1928, a nurse named Marian Bridgette bought the building and, along with her sister Margaret Del Rosso, another nurse, turned it into a convalescent home for people with tuberculosis. Marian continued her work until 1955, when a heart attack left her weakened and unable to take in patients. She died in the home in 1973.

While running the convalescent center, Mrs. B, as she came to be known, made a habit of walking the halls at night to close doors, turn off lights and check in on her patients. So that explained the late-night ramblings and nurturing energy. Frank even had a "chat" with Mrs. B to ask her to keep the nocturnal noises to a minimum. "I explained to Marian that we want her to live here as long as she wants to, but at night she needs to be quiet so our guests can sleep." It appears she listened because there is much less activity now. Frank notes, "She is a lot more active when the house is empty."

But what of the other not-so-friendly entities? Frank brought in a shaman to perform a clearing ceremony. The woman stated that there were a lot of active spirits in the house and that in addition to Mrs. B, she picked up on a benign and generally inactive spirit called the Colonel. The shaman also told Frank that Marian often protected him from some unfriendly entities, including the one in the basement. "She's apparently happy that I'm here taking care of the house," says Frank. The shamanic clear-out seems to have done the trick because the basement is now just a storage area, without the nasty nauseating energy, and most of the other random negative sensations are also gone.

That leaves Mrs. B. Aside from the assistance in tidying up—closing drawers, shutting doors—some guests have seen her sitting in the garden now and then. "We have pictures of Marian supplied by her granddaughter who still lives in Asheville," says Frank. So when a guest recently inquired about the elderly woman with the gray hair pulled up, Frank brought out a picture of Mrs. B. The guest confirmed that Mrs. B was the person enjoying a moment of morning serenity in the garden.

Ralph is the skeptic of the pair. Frank laughs, "He says to me, 'Sure you had a shaman come in and do a clearing, but all she cleared was your wallet.'" However, even Ralph admits there is something odd about the inn, and though it might not qualify as a ghost, because after all you have to believe in ghosts for that to happen, there is *something*.

So if you happen to be traveling through the splendid valleys of North Carolina's mountains, stop by the 1889 WhiteGate Inn for an idyllic rest with a not-so-idle ghost.

The 1927 Lake Lure Inn and Spa
Lake Lure, North Carolina

The 1927 Lake Lure Inn and Spa has an illustrious past; built as a resort for the wealthy, it also served as a site for soldiers to recuperate during World War II. Names such as F. Scott Fitzgerald, Franklin D. Roosevelt and Emily Post once graced the roster of guests. The hallways are filled with historic photographs and paintings that date back to the days when a doctor in search of the therapeutic airs of North Carolina's "Thermal Belt" stopped to admire the view. It is easy to see why so many people who come here feel that the spirits of the past continue to reside at the inn.

It was the turn of the 20th century when Dr. Lucius B. Morse traveled through Hickory Nut Gorge, North Carolina, on a mission to find a climate that might cure his tuberculosis. The doctor from Missouri was so entranced by the monolithic Chimney Rock that towers over the nearby gorge that he rode a donkey to the top to view the entire region. From that vantage point, Dr. Morse envisioned the development of a lake and resort community—it would become an all-consuming passion into which he put all his energy until he died.

In 1925, Dr. Morse and his two brothers Hiram and Asahel created the Carolina Mountain Power Company and built a dam on the Broad River at Tumbling Shoals to create the lake that National Geographic has called "one of the most beautiful man-made lakes in the world." It was Dr. Morse's wife, Elizabeth Parkenson, who came up with the name Lake

Lure. Overlooking the 27 miles of shoreline, Dr. Morse built an inn with the idea of creating a year-round resort that would enjoy the spectacular views of beautiful mountains and granite cliffs.

Dr. Morse's inn opened in 1927 just as the waters of the newly formed lake reached their peak. But the economic collapse in 1929 and the ensuing Great Depression stalled the resort development until the mid-1960s, when the Town of Lake Lure acquired the lake and its recreational facilities. Dr. Morse had died in July 1946 of tuberculosis and never saw his dream completely fulfilled, but he never left the Blue Ridge Mountain area—and he may still be there in spirit.

Many of the staff members at the 1927 Lake Lure Inn feel sure that Dr. Morse has been seen and heard in the spa area located in the basement. Night auditors have reported seeing a male figure that resembles Dr. Morse standing by the fireplace in the dining room. One employee working alone in the spa doing laundry heard a man with a low, gravelly voice call her name as she walked through—she dropped the linens and ran. And one supervisor who went to the washroom because she felt ill heard someone ask if she was all right. She turned to reply, but there was no one else in the room. Could it be a case of once a doctor, always a doctor—even in the afterlife?

Most of the stories of inexplicable occurrences center around three areas in the hotel: the spa, the dining room and room 218, where a murder took place many years ago. Interestingly, all three areas are in a straight vertical line, one above the other.

The tale of the murdered bride dates back to the 1930s. As the story goes, the bliss of a newly wedded couple turned sour just hours after the ceremony at the wedding reception. There was a heated exchange of words because the groom had the impression that his new wife had been unfaithful. The newlyweds returned to their room, but the husband could not subdue his rage and killed his bride before taking his own life. Guests have reported hearing the faint cries of a woman resonate throughout the hotel.

All the reports of mysterious incidents got the attention of Joe Wright and his newly formed team, Paranormal Scene Investigators. In addition to tales of the ghostly bride and phantom physician, they had heard eyewitness reports of televisions turning on and off or changing channels, beds unmaking themselves and kitchen staff being pushed on the rear staircase by the pantry. In 2006, fueled by "an overwhelming need to seek out the truth," the group visited the 1927 Lake Lure Inn for the first of many investigations.

Joe takes his investigations seriously. "We're meticulous with our evidence. It is hard for me to take some things seriously because I find short attention spans or excitement of the moment causes confusion, and details are lost." Joe relies on modern technology to record things invisible or inaudible to humans, and by removing the "human" element can use the results to try to explain the inexplicable. "We depend on science," says Joe, "and we look for all possible explanations before concluding there is a paranormal phenomenon."

Armed with state-of-the-art audio and video surveillance equipment plus a barometric pressure station, the team set up in the hotel's hot spots: room 218 and the spa. "The Lake Lure Inn would meet and exceed everything we had hoped for," writes Joe in the final report. Over the course of the night, the team heard several sounds and located some unusual cold spots, but the highlight was an audio recording caught on tape just after midnight in room 218.

The women in the group had just settled in to spend the rest of the night in the room when "a disembodied scream rang out." The sound shocked the investigators. "Not only was it heard by everyone in the room," reports Joe, "but it was also caught on two different recorders." It was not clear to the investigators if the scream coincided with the timing of the actual murder decades ago, or if it was meant to evoke sympathy from the women who heard it. "This would suggest an intelligence which is rare," says Joe. "In either case we had it, and it was going to be hard to explain away."

In a second investigation in 2007, the team recorded an electronic voice phenomenon (EVP) of a woman's scream that was the same as the first. "It was identical in length and tone," says Joe in an interview for the *Daily Courier*. "If you played the two of them side by side you would say they were recorded the same way. So we have exactly the same scream, which kind of rules out that there was anybody wandering the halls that screamed during the last investigation."

But back to the initial investigation—the night was not yet over. Before packing up to go home, the PSI team recorded another voice that would not be discovered until days later when going through all the recordings. "One of the best EVPs captured at the Lake Lure Inn appeared as several pops and cracks. After it was enhanced, filtered and then amplified, it was clearly a voice saying, 'Get the hell out, Sparky.' What makes this a solid piece of evidence is that the investigator performing the EVP sweep is named Sparky."

When the team returned for its second investigation, it set up in the spa, room 218 and this time in room 318 to explore a "straight line" theory postulated by Joe Wright. "If the hotel was built on a shifting foundation of specific minerals, it could create a magnetic field emanating upward," he postulates. "This being the case, then we should get activity in 318 as well. And we did!"

In addition to sounds recorded in rooms 218 and 318, the team had another inexplicable event on record. Just after midnight, a table in the spa moved out from the wall and up against one of the stationary cameras on a tripod. The table was out of the camera's line of vision, but the sound of the table moving can clearly be heard on the audio. At the time, the spa was empty.

"My belief is, if in fact there is a magnetic field in these locations," summarizes Joe, "then it may be trapping the entities and in return allowing them to feed from it and grow strong enough to manifest. Or maybe it's just a coincidence. Either way, it left us scratching our heads and wondering."

In February 2009, the team revisited the inn as part of a paranormal conference. Although Joe did not have the opportunity to conduct a full investigation, there was an opportunity to gather more data. One of the PSI team members spent the night in room 217, next to where they heard the scream. Rooms 217 and 218 used to be one large room, and there are reports of unusual things in both. The investigator reported being awakened by something in the middle of the night, and as he sat up in bed he saw a face in the corner by the doorway. "He just saw the outline of a person's head and maybe shoulders," says Joe. "Unfortunately he didn't have his camera ready to go, so he spent the rest of the night trying to shoot something but didn't manage to capture it digitally."

As well, another PSI team member saw a shadow of a person pass by a curtain down in the spa area. The investigator immediately jumped up and checked the other side of the curtain, but there was no one visible.

And for the first time, the investigators were allowed access to the neighboring arcade building, which was used as a hospital for soldiers during World War II. The inn and the pavilion, as it is called, were joined by an underground tunnel that was boarded up many years ago. While on the second floor, one team member took a remarkable photo of an apparition using a full-spectrum camera that can detect a wider spectrum of light, including infrared and ultraviolet light. The picture clearly shows a figure in a doorway. It stunned everyone who saw it.

"We definitely feel more investigation is warranted," says Joe. The PSI team intends to return to both the inn and the pavilion to conduct more studies.

Current owners George and Hope Wittmer are enjoying this facet of their inn. After extensive renovations, they now feel that the hotel is just the right blend of the elegance of the past and the modern sophistication of the present. Toss in a few ghosts, and there is something for everyone to enjoy.

The High Hampton Inn

Cashiers, North Carolina

A haven of southern hospitality doesn't normally boast screeching white owls with human spirits, haunted springs that prevent people from leaving or cottages with unseen piano-playing phantoms. So leave it to the High Hampton Inn and Country Club near Cashiers, North Carolina, to break with tradition. Sipping mint juleps on the deck becomes a whole new experience when shared with ghosts.

The High Hampton is a large, privately owned resort stretching across 1400 acres of mountainous landscape that once belonged to Confederate General Wade Hampton, who also served as governor of South Carolina and later as a U.S. senator. Considered one of the wealthiest men in the region, he built the High Hampton estate in 1850 and used it as his summer home until his death in 1902.

Dr. William Halsted, the chief surgeon at Baltimore's John Hopkins Hospital, married the general's niece and purchased the property after being entranced by the beauty of the hills. When Dr. Halsted and his wife died (both in 1922) they left no heirs, so the land went up for sale. The McKee clan bought the estate and built a two-story inn, golf course and tennis courts. It has been open to the public since 1922.

The first ghost story emerged when General Hampton was still alive. His nephew by marriage, Dr. Halsted, wanted to buy land for a summer estate and set his sights on a piece of land adjacent to the Hampton estate that was owned by

Hannibal Heaton. Halsted offered Heaton $1600 to hand over the deed to the property. Mark Jones, one of the current managers on the property, gives historical talks to guests interested in the local lore. "There are two versions of this story," he says.

The version most commonly told is the following. Hannibal Heaton wanted to take the offer and sell, but his wife stubbornly refused to part with the land. Loesa Emmalie stood firm. Mark Jones recounts the tale. "She threatened Hannibal Heaton, saying, 'If you sell my property to the people at the High Hampton, I'll kill myself.'"

Hannibal sold the land, assuming his wife's threats were idle—big mistake. He arrived home with money and a bill of sale, but his wife no longer cared. Loesa Emmalie had hanged herself from a tree in the yard. When the distraught Hannibal tried to get her down, there was a white owl flying around and screeching at him. He was forced to ask his neighbors for help to get his wife's body down from the tree.

According to the local lore, Hannibal's hair turned white almost overnight. The owl refused to leave the tree, screeching and hooting throughout the night. Convinced that his wife (who had had white hair from an early age) had turned into the owl, Hannibal never spent any of the money from the sale of the property; he went off into the woods and was never seen again. When the original High Hampton burned down in 1932 and was rebuilt, the resort guests claimed to see a white owl flying among the trees or hear its piercing screech after dark.

Mark says the second version of the story came to light when he was speaking at the local public library. "A historian came up after hearing me recite the former version and corrected me. She pulled out an 1898 press release that confirmed the hanging but stated that Loesa hanged herself in a barn, not a tree. The article also said that Hannibal moved to Franklin, North Carolina, where he is buried. He did get to spend the money and lived out his life with his family."

Although the owl may have been a barn owl, Mark still hears guests say that they felt the spirit of Loesa circle overhead. "A lot of people tell me they've seen the white owl flying around the estate. I tell them we do have white squirrels—not albino but a kind of white squirrel—and then suggest that perhaps they spent too much time in the tavern," he laughs.

There is a haunted spring on the property that was used by Indians and by the travelers who passed through. The estate grounds are on a path from Cashiers to South Carolina, and back in the days when people went by trail, they would stop and rest at the spring before embarking on the last leg of the journey. "One of our maintenance men unearthed the spring and a rock wall with some masonry work done to make it more accessible," Mark tells me. "The story is that if you drink water from the spring, you can't leave High Hampton. Now, we've had people leave to work elsewhere, but they come back. We joke that we slip people some water, and that's how we get our fifth-generation guests here." Mark confides that he never drank the water when he started at the inn because he feared it came from the spring.

Amusing as those tales are, Mark's voice changes when he talks about the *real* ghosts at the inn. "There is a particular cottage with mischievous entities. Guests can't sleep, cabinets open, and a piano plays by itself."

Thorpe Cottage was built during World War II and is named after a man who worked with the Department of Defense. He arranged a deal that would bring power to the area if he could build a place on the property. The government wanted to put power lines through for making aluminum at a nearby production plant; they needed the power to extract the aluminum out of bauxite shipped up from Jamaica. After Thorpe divorced his wife, Mr. McKee bought the cottage back, and it re-entered the High Hampton properties in 1960s. It's not clear when the ghost moved in.

Mark Jones worked as a bellman in 1987. "I was preparing a function at this cottage, and the maintenance superintendent wouldn't go in without someone with him." The man, named Irving, told Mark the place was haunted. Irving explained the reason behind his unease. On a different occasion, Irving had spent hours taking all the books off the cottage shelves—books that date back to the early 1940s—boxing them and carting them to storage. The cottage was closed so that it could be redecorated. But the next morning, Irving got a call. All the books had somehow returned to the shelves overnight. "He just totally believed there was some kind of spirit in there," says Mark.

Sue Bumgarner, the same woman who was accosted at the Library Club (see page 81), used to work at the High Hampton and had her own run-in with the supernatural at Thorpe Cottage. Sue tells me, "I used to check in the afternoons that housekeeping had done their job. I went to Thorpe Cottage to give it a once-over. While I was inspecting one of the bedrooms, the piano in the living room started playing—and it's not a player piano either!" Sue left and got a bellman to go back into the cottage with her. "He said, 'I don't want to go,' and I said, 'Yes, you are.' We both went, and as we checked the rooms the piano started playing again." The bellman came out into the living room and said, "I thought you were playing—" Sue cut him off, saying she didn't know how to play. "Who's playing it then?" asked the bellman. The two then hurried out the door. "And I said I will never go back there," says Sue, who admits she rarely tells people about this experience. "We're all a bit reluctant to talk about it because people think we're crazy."

Some guests staying in the cottage have voiced concerns about the presence of an unseen entity. Mark Jones says that at the time, the guests did not know anything of the inn's haunted history. One family just couldn't sleep at night. Something kept them awake, and it got to the point that they insisted on moving or they would check out and leave. After they switched to another cottage, everything was fine. There wasn't anything specific on which they could blame the sleepless nights, just a strange feeling while inside the cottage.

Then there is the time that a guest came over to the main house visibly upset, stating that someone in the cottage had offended his wife by cursing loudly and banging about in the kitchen area. Thorpe Cottage is built with four bedrooms off a common sitting area, so several guests often share it. It is also the only cottage to have a kitchen because the original owner lived there. Most guests at the High Hampton Inn eat their meals in the dining room. The elderly male guest explained to Mark that they heard a man swearing and opening cupboards in the kitchen. The profanity compelled him to go out and confront the person, but the kitchen was empty. However, all the drawers and cupboard doors stood open.

Upon hearing this, Mark called the maintenance man on the radio and had him drive over immediately, thinking they would catch any trespasser looking for food because there was no way off the property without being seen. "He didn't find a thing," says Mark. "He looked all over and there was no one in sight." Mark admits that there might be a non-paranormal explanation: it is possible that a person ran off through the brush. But then he tells his own story of supernatural high jinks out at Thorpe Cottage.

"I was setting up the bar on the front deck for a party," he begins. "It was about 4:30 PM, and I was waiting for the catered food to arrive." Mark was also to be a guest of the function, so once he had the bar set up, he thought he might observe the onset of happy hour. Says Mark, "I thought it was time for a cocktail." The problem was, he wasn't alone. "Housekeeping had been coming over to clean up rooms in case a guest needed to stay over. I could hear housekeepers talking. I thought, shoot, I can't have a drink in front of staff." Mark had half a dozen bags of ice, so while he waited for the cleaning staff to finish, he set to work banging the ice on the deck to loosen it up. "When I finished the last bag, emptied the ice into the cooler and put the bag in the trash, a few minutes passed and I realized no one was talking. I went inside—no one was there. Then I saw all the vans were gone—and remembered they had left about 15 minutes before."

Was he hearing things? Mark says no. "There were two female voices. I could hear them talking but could not make out what they said. I clearly heard the two voices, and I was sober. When I tried to listen in they would lower their voices, but when I banged the ice the voices got louder."

Word of the happenings at Thorpe Cottage soon got around. Asheville-born paranormal investigator Joshua P. Warren brought his "gadgets and gizmos" to the High Hampton and apparently picked up strong readings inside the cottage. He also took a picture in one of the bedroom mirrors, and the image revealed a woman wearing a 1940s-style hat. "It was a strange thing to see," says Mark. "Maybe it was the silhouette of one of the ladies I heard talking."

The High Hampton sits at an elevation of 3600 feet and prides itself on eschewing all electronic devices such as telephones, computers and televisions. Mark proudly tells people that he is fourth-generation Jackson County. "We have third-generation staff, people who worked here 22 years and two staff members here 50 years. And we have fifth-generation guests. Some of us are fortunate that we didn't have to leave." Add to that an old property, a few deaths over the years and the mysterious mountain air, and it all creates a serenely supernatural setting. It's no wonder the spirits stick around too.

The Inn on Main Street

Weaverville, North Carolina

In the long shadows of the Blue Ridge Mountains, the town of Weaverville keeps a pace of life more in tune with centuries past. People rarely lock their doors. A fireworks display on the Fourth of July stops traffic. And you can hear the crowds cheering at the Little League games more than a block away. Travelers who discover its charms say it feels like coming home. Perhaps that explains why some of the original residents continue to linger, reluctant to leave this mountain retreat.

Dan and Nancy Ward are the innkeepers of the Inn on Main Street, a pale blue and white-trimmed Victorian home that epitomizes country elegance. After almost 11 years living at the inn, Dan Ward says that now more than ever he feels like a caretaker rather than an owner—in large part because of the spirits that still roam around the premises. "This house has been around twice as long as I have, so when you do encounter these spirits, it reinforces the sense that I am going to come and go, but there are spirits here who will outlast me and watch over the house. It's very comforting."

The house was built by Dr. Zebulon Vance Robinson early in the 1900s. There is no exact date because record-keeping in those days wasn't rigorous, so town officials simply entered 1900 as a rough estimate. Doc Robinson lived in the upper stories of the home with his family and had his office and surgery on the main floor. The parlor to the right of the front door was the waiting room. Not all Dr. Robinson's patients survived surgery; Dan figures there were a few deaths over the years. And the good doctor himself passed away in the 1920s, which is more spiritual fodder for the house.

In the years between Doc Robinson and the Wards, the home was used as a school, a ministerial student residence and a summer guesthouse for tourists. It became a bed and breakfast in 1991, and the Wards took ownership in 1998. "Our first encounter of a strange kind was early on," says Dan. "It was our first or second New Year's Eve. We were in the parlor having a toast with a few friends when we heard what sounded like a picture falling off the wall in the next room." Dan went to see what had crashed to the floor, but nothing was amiss. "I thought, that it was strange, and rejoined the party."

A little while later another crash resounded from the same room. Again there was nothing wrong. Dan says, "At some point close to midnight, we all heard the back door open and close, followed by the sound of someone walking around." Dan and Nancy knew that all the guests going out to celebrate had left already, and they were not expecting anyone else to join their party. Dan explored down the hall, but no one had entered the house. He looked outside, and no one had left it either. "I thought, that's pretty peculiar. And then I didn't think much of it again for a while."

Soon enough, Dan realized that the mysterious sounds that night might have been the resident spirits' way of saying hello, because the next thing to occur was the soft sound of a lady's voice calling from the main floor while he worked upstairs. "Back when we first bought the inn, I was here alone a lot doing maintenance while Nancy was out earning enough money for us to pay the bills," explains Dan. "I was upstairs hauling a bucket around cleaning the bathrooms, and I would hear someone yoo-hooing from downstairs as if they had come in and saw no one was around so they wanted to see if anyone was home." Dan, of course, would run downstairs to answer the call and—that's right—no one was ever there. He might have written it off as wayward breezes or too many cleaning fumes, but guests at the inn hear the voices too.

People over the years have commented at breakfast that they heard a lady or perhaps a few ladies whispering in the Lee Room, a first-floor guest room named after the Confederate general. The voice is soft and feminine but indistinct. It is not clear who she is talking to, whether it is to herself, to others or to the guests listening in on the ethereal sound. One female guest claimed to have seen the source of the whispering voice. She told Dan that she saw the figure of a pleasant-looking woman in the mirror as she put on her makeup. Seeing the spectral shape did not scare the guest, who apparently had seen spirits before. Dan says no one has been spooked by the spirit. "No one has ever felt threatened. It's all quite benign."

Hearing a whispering voice is the most common occurrence at the inn, but there are others of note. Very early in the Wards' time as owners, they had a deeply religious couple stay. Dan recalls that they were quite concerned about a passage in the Old Testament that had to do with the idea that where blood is spilled, evil will linger. The pair was distraught about a bloodstain they observed in one of the bathrooms and went upstairs to pray about it. In the morning, they came down to tell Dan that they prayed until 3 AM and finally got a message that the house has nothing but happy spirits. "So in a way we got the 'Good Housekeeping Seal of Approval,'" says Dan, summing that one up.

Another guest came to stay with her granddaughter and told Dan that she was from a long line of women of Cherokee blood with the sixth sense. "I didn't tell them anything about the spirits we had observed or the history of the house," says Dan, "but when they left they gave me a run-down of what they experienced." The woman thought Dan would like to know that several spirits lingered around the laundry area, but she did not know why that might be. "She didn't realize that that's where the doctor's surgery used to be," Dan says. "She made a point of saying there are a lot of them, though, all hanging around."

Dan has another experience that he feels may confirm the presence of Doc Robinson's spirit. He begins, "The only time that Nancy and I overtly encountered what we thought was off the realm of what you could expect was when we had guys come in to put in gas fireplaces." In order to convert the original fireplaces into gas, they had to put vents in old chimneys. One of the workmen tried to put pipe in from the roof, but the pipe wouldn't budge. "The fellow got out a crowbar and started banging. That's when we discovered there was plug of concrete in there. It fell out and blew dust all over the rooms." Dan and Nancy now had a huge mess to clean up in the Ayers Room—the room that Doc Robinson once occupied.

"We were busy cleaning and scrubbing, and we turned the TV on," says Dan. The problem was that the television would change the channel by itself. "It would change to Turner Classic Movies, settling on *The Magnificent Ambersons* [a period piece set in 1873], and I had the feeling that the doctor was upset by all the soot in the room." Dan pursued the strange experience, asking around as to what might cause the television to spontaneously change channels. People suggested it could be signals from the local fire station or a garage door opener affecting the television's remote control. Dan might have accepted that, but the unusual channel changing didn't continue. "Once it was cleaned up, everything returned to normal in the Ayers Room."

Dan grew up in Illinois and moved to North Carolina in the 1970s. He's heard a lot of strange things and knows that people like to tell ghost stories. But as far as he and Nancy are concerned, the spirits in their bed and breakfast are best left on their own. "I think things only get stirred up when there are things that are out of the status quo." Dan adds, "I don't think we have conscious souls. It is more like echoes of energy, like when you dip an oar in water and get the water swirling. When we interrupt the energy, that's when the swirling stops and the water smacks against the side of the canoe, to continue the metaphor."

Dan has a take on the spirit entities that share his home: "What we have is not a good or bad ghost, just an echo of harmonious, happy energy. Not a bunch of unsettled souls looking to mix it up with the living world."

The Wards don't know if the spirits are connected to the people who lived there or who died there. And they don't care. Several paranormal investigative teams "with all the electronic gizmos" have approached them about the stories circulating, but the Wards are not interested in having the "ghost busters" set up to gather data. "I imagine someone might be able to figure out who the whispering lady is," admits Dan, "but really, why?"

Although Dan doesn't want to encourage people to come looking for ghosts, he is eager for people to experience the comforting sense of spiritual caretaking that coincides nicely with how the Wards run their business. Guests are treated to organically grown food from their garden, and most of the delicious baked goods served for breakfast are made from scratch. So, the quiet, slow-paced lifestyle of a bygone era lives on at the Inn on Main Street...and if you're lucky, you may catch a glimpse or hear a snippet from those who lived it a century ago.

The Highlands Inn

Highlands, North Carolina

Sabrina Hawkins doesn't know for sure who haunts her historic inn, nor does she really want to know. She has not personally experienced any of the numerous encounters guests and employees report, and, she says, "I don't want to."

Sabrina does admit, however, that there is something strange that stays on at the Highlands Inn even when everyone else has checked out or gone home for the night. "My mother and my children don't like to walk through the inn alone at night," says Sabrina. "They say it's too spooky."

Megan Miller, owner of the Library Club and no stranger to ghostly goings-on herself (see page 81), can attest to the presence of something paranormal at the Highlands. "I spent a night there not long ago," she says, "and I knew that the inn was rumored to be haunted. The story is that a woman walks across the room from the window to the door and disappears."

The story to which Megan refers involves room 34 of the inn. So she stayed there, not sure what to expect. "That night I was awakened by a clanking sound. I assumed it was ice in the ice bucket melting and hitting the metal somehow, but when I turned on the light, my car keys had moved two feet from where I put them."

Other guests have also been victims of the entity's pranks. One woman told Sabrina that she put her heart medication on the night table before falling asleep so that she could easily reach it in the middle of the night when she needed to take more. However, the bottle was not there when she went to find it. In the daylight, she searched throughout the room, under the bed, in her bags, and could not find the medicine. Later that day, cleaning staff found the pills beneath the bed of the room one floor below room 34.

But the best evidence that the Highlands Inn holds an energy from beyond is an eyewitness account recorded on the hotel's website and in Stephanie Burt Williams' book *Haunted Hills: Ghosts and Legends of Highlands and Cashiers, North Carolina.*

Tammy Steele and her husband checked into room 34 of the Highlands Inn for an autumnal retreat, some quiet time to enjoy the fall colors and crisp mountain air. On the Saturday night, after a day of walking around, Tammy returned to the room to change for dinner. She sat on the edge of her bed to take off her boots, and as she bent over to tug them off, she felt a sudden deep chill as if the window were open. Tammy looked up expecting either to see the window ajar or that her husband had returned, and instead found herself face to face with a young woman.

The woman seemed unaware of Tammy's presence. Dressed in late 19th- or early 20th-century garb and with her brown tresses bundled up on top of her head, the figure looked almost solid, according to Tammy. She walked from the window toward the door, and as she did so, her figure became more and more transparent until she faded out of sight. It was hard to say if the woman passed through the door or simply vanished.

Later that same evening, after enjoying a large meal, Tammy could not sleep so she sat up watching television while her husband slept. In the dimly lit room, something caught Tammy's eye from near the window, and her eyes made out a dark shadow. "I felt the hairs on my arms stand up and I got another chill," reports Tammy. The shadow traveled the same path as the female ghost—from window to door—then disappeared.

On Sunday, it was Tammy's husband's turn to experience the room's unregistered guest. As they packed to leave, Tammy's husband jumped out of the closet and darted to the mirror. He told Tammy he felt something move slowly down the back of his neck—a woman's finger perhaps?—and checked in the mirror to see if it was a bug crawling inside his shirt—no bug, and no idea what it was.

So who might the mysterious ghost guest be? The best guess is that it is a former owner, Miss Helen Major.

Highlands Inn was built at over 4000 feet above sea level back in 1880 by Joseph Halleck to provide relief from the summer heat for those people living in the sweltering lowlands. Every year, the well-to-do plantation owners and business people packed into horse-drawn carriages to make the trek through the Blue Ridge Mountains to the Highlands Inn plateau. The inn passed through a few hands before being purchased by a Canadian woman named Helen Major in 1969.

Miss Major's passion was food. According to Sabrina Hawkins, it was Miss Major's prowess in the kitchen that created the inn's reputation as a place of fine dining. The former owner spent much of her day in the kitchen, turning out three meals a day for guests. That may explain why most of the recent unusual activity takes place in the kitchen.

Sabrina's mother has heard clanking pots and has seen lights turn on and off when the kitchen is empty. "My mother stays overnight at the inn during low season so there is some-one on hand to help the guests," Sabrina explains. "One night after all the lights had been turned off, she heard a pot bang-ing in the kitchen. It was late, sometime after midnight. She went to investigate, and there was a light on. So the next morning she asked the guests if anyone had been down to the kitchen, but they all said they had gone to bed early that night. My mom was terrified because she knew something was in that kitchen."

Another clue to the spirit's identity could be in the distinc-tive odor of popcorn. Miss Major loved to eat it, and guests often report the unmistakable scent of freshly popped corn wafting through the rooms near where she lived at the inn. "I have smelled the popcorn," admits Sabrina. "And one of my housekeepers found a piece of popcorn under the bed and was a little spooked."

Is Miss Major's spirit locked in some sort of eternal loop in room 34? Or is it the remnant energy of another guest or owner from the early days at the inn, spinning in a timeless rut, destined to tread the path from window to door forever? In such a lovely setting, it is easy to see why there is no urgency to change course. But if you choose to stay in room 34, remember to keep an eye on your keys and stay clear of the doorway.

The Martha Washington Inn
Abingdon, Virginia

"There are a few ghost stories that float around, and we have some workers who have felt or seen things," says general manager Christopher Lowe. Although he doesn't believe any of the tales, Lowe says that the Martha Washington Inn—nicknamed the Martha—is well known for some tragic ghosts, most from the Civil War era, including a young girl who still pines for her dead soldier and a bloodstain that reappears on the spot where a Confederate soldier was shot and killed. When you consider that Abingdon is the oldest town in the United States west of the Blue Ridge Mountains, it isn't a huge stretch to assume that it may have some of the oldest ghosts in the country too.

All that seems a lifetime away when one is inside the lavish historic hotel and spa, which sits nestled amid lush, rolling hills. It seems more reasonable to contemplate a pedicure than a phantom. However, this building is inextricably linked to the history of this Appalachian enclave, and violence, bloodshed and death often beget ghosts.

Virginia General Francis Preston built the $15,000 home in 1832 for his wife Sarah and their nine children. The private residence changed hands in 1858 and became a finishing school for young girls. Three years later, with the outbreak of the Civil War, the building served as a hospital for wounded soldiers. One of the more romantic ghost stories emerges from this pairing of functions, because not all the girls left for home during the war; some volunteered to stay and nurse the injured men.

After the Civil War, the Martha became a women's college. Then in 1935, two years after the equally haunted Barter Theatre opened across the street and right in the middle of the Great Depression, it opened as a hotel. There were ups and downs; it was owned by a group of 10 or 12 businessmen in the 1970s, but infighting and costs forced them to sell. In 1984, the United Company bought the property and undertook a massive $8 million renovation. Eleven years later it became part of a collection of privately owned historic properties. The spa opened in February 2006 to add to the glamour.

Back to the ghosts. Nearly 150 years after the Civil War began, its first casualties still haunt the inn. The most enduring and endearing of the ghosts is that of a lovesick girl who is seen ascending the steps to the room in which her sweetheart died. According to the lore the ghost's name is Beth Anne Smith. The young girl nursed Captain John Stoves, a fatally wounded officer—in some stories he's a Confederate and in others a Yankee—who had been carried up to the third floor of the converted school to a large dormitory room. In addition to cleaning the soldier's wounds, Beth sang and played violin for Stoves.

Beth fell in love with the dying officer, but her sentiment could not save Stoves. The story goes that he asked her to play something for him in the moments before he died, telling her he knew his time had come. Beth played a melody for the captain on her violin, though he may not have lived long enough to hear it.

In a sad denouement, Beth died soon after, a victim of either scarlet or typhoid fever. Her heartfelt melodies can still be heard by guests and staff late at night on the third floor, a tribute to the eternal nature of her love for the soldier. Some people claim to have seen her apparition climbing the steps in her purple apron dress as if still on her way to tend to the captain's wounds.

The reappearing bloodstain is another Civil War–era reminder of the violence that ensued in the name of democracy. This time a Confederate soldier was shot by Union officers in front of his lady love. The young man's blood stained the floor before he could be carried away, and all efforts to remove the stain failed. Even when washed away, the gruesome dark stain reappeared relentlessly on the floor outside what is now the Governor's Suite until the hotel finally covered the patch with carpet. One bellhop claims that even putting something down to cover the spot has not worked and that carpets develop holes over the area where the soldier died.

A few other ghosts are said to haunt various areas of the hotel. There is a phantom horse that appears outside by the front steps. The horse, loyal to a Union soldier who was killed in 1864, continues to roam the grounds as if searching for its master. Some reports exist of seeing the apparition of a badly wounded soldier hobbling along on a crutch—the unusual aspect of this ghost is that it leaves a trail of mud behind it as it moves down the hallway. And an underground tunnel that used to join the Martha Washington Inn with the Barter Theatre (see page 101) is said to house an awful spirit, something very nasty that is never seen but can be felt as an evil or angry presence. No one knows for sure who the spiteful specter might be, though theories range from a man who died in a tunnel collapse to a Confederate soldier who got caught smuggling ammunition out of the inn's basement.

One guest saw what may have been the very clear apparition of a soldier while visiting in March 2007. The man, who posted his experience in a blog under the name TTatum on December 26, 2007, explains that on Sunday, March 4, he and his wife got separated after breakfast in the basement café, so he walked toward the front stairway to find her. He says, "As I came up the hallway headed toward the front stairway, I looked down the back stair hallway and saw what I thought was a Civil War reenactor standing at the foot of the back stairway staring into the gift shop, which was closed. He was a small-framed, bearded man with gray hair wearing a beautiful teal-gray Confederate dress uniform."

Struck by the beauty of the uniform, the man turned around and went back to the hallway for a closer look, but there was no one there. Intent on seeing the costume again, the man says, "I hurried past the stairway to see if he had gone into the restaurant. He wasn't there. So I turned and hurried up the stairs. He was nowhere to be found.

"I'm not sure I saw an apparition, but it was odd. I was probably 15 feet from him, to his right. I didn't see him walk through any walls or vanish. He just looked out of place because there were no Civil War reenactments in the area. And it was 10 AM on a cold March Sunday morning."

After seven years at the helm of the Martha, Christopher Lowe says he hasn't seen anything to convince him that the stories are true and doesn't actively market that aspect of this luxury inn, but he admits that you can't squelch a good story. Perhaps a visit to this picturesque part of the world is in order—after all, what better reason to spend a day at a spa than to say that it is part of a spiritual quest?

3
Entertaining Haunts

The Greenbrier Restaurant

Gatlinburg, Tennessee

The legend of the Greenbrier ghost is well known in the Smokies. It's one of those stories the locals don't think much about, having grown up with it, until confronted by Lydia or one of many other spirits roaming the restaurant. Just ask the owners.

Becky Hadden's first words to me were, "Oh, we have *lots* of stories." They have also had at least four paranormal research groups cart in all their recording gear to try to get a lock on what exactly there is for spirit life in the former lodge.

Becky, husband David and son Jordan now own the Greenbrier Restaurant. They took over from David's parents, who ran the facility from 1980 to 1993. The main log structure initially functioned as a hunting lodge back in the 1930s. Original owner Blanche Moffat took in travelers and holiday-seekers as well, and treated them to her southern hospitality by serving up a big breakfast each morning before they set out to explore the area. The lodge boasted the first concrete swimming pool in Gatlinburg, another draw for people wanting a mountain retreat.

The romantic setting made the lodge a natural choice for honeymooners—and that's where the story of Lydia begins. She lived at the lodge, one of the young, single women who boarded with Mrs. Moffat, and she fell in love with a handsome young man who eventually asked for her hand in marriage. Her wedding day arrived, and Lydia joyfully prepared to declare "I do." However, her betrothed did not show up at the church. After hours of expectant waiting, Lydia gave up hope. The rejected bride returned to the lodge, where she climbed to the second floor and hanged herself from a ceiling beam.

Only a few days after Lydia's suicide, the groom-to-be was found dead in the Smoky Mountains, apparently the victim of a wild mountain cat. Some locals speculated that Lydia's spirit sought out the young man, and when she found him, she turned into a cat and killed him out of revenge for her wedding day humiliation. Of course, that is just imaginative conjecture. It may well be that the poor man died before he was able to marry the lovely Lydia. Regardless, Lydia's restless spirit continues to make life interesting for the owners and guests of the restaurant.

A lodge caretaker had many sleepless nights because of Lydia's tormented spirit. Cries of "Mark my grave!" kept the poor man awake for nights on end until he finally realized that eternity took on a whole new meaning when it was a ghost clamoring for attention. He finally did as requested, going out and hammering a wooden cross into the unmarked ground where he believed Lydia to be buried, and the night-time commotion ceased.

Sitting above the fireplace is a remarkable photograph. Dean Hadden, Dave's father, found it in a dresser drawer in the room that had been Blanche Moffat's bedroom. Becky thinks the photo is actually from a very brief time in the 1970s when the restaurant was operated as a fancy French dining room. The picture is of a woman who appears to fade away below the waist as she walks through a doorway from the kitchen into the lobby area. "All you can see is a white blur," says Becky, "but though it's a woman's body, you can see a man's face reflected in one of the copper pots." Is it Lydia—proof that her ghost stays connected to the place in which she died? Or is it just a faded picture?

The East Tennessee Paranormal Research Society favors the former option. The group spent several hours in the restaurant in January 2007 with digital cameras and audio recording devices, asking whatever spirits might be present to speak to them. When they listened to their recordings later, the ETPRS claims to have captured several electronic voice phenomena (EVPs). In other words, the spirit or spirits spoke. One recording in particular is held up as evidence that Lydia remains on the premises. Investigator Donna Dudley sat in the dining room and told Lydia out loud that she would be happy to hear from her. The response caught on tape is a voice whispering, "Then I'm not dead."

"Her contacting me directly was really impressive," says Donna, who has conducted numerous investigations for ETPRS. Donna and her husband Marshall feel sure there is more than one spirit at the Greenbrier, given the number of "voices" they recorded during their visit. The audio recordings can all be heard on the organization's website.

Becky Hadden isn't sure who the other spirits might be but says her teenaged son Jordan has seen a female ghost a few times, though more so when he was much younger. "When Jordan was six years old, he was watching TV while I was doing up the bar order and Dave was cleaning up at the end of the day. He called to his dad a few times, then he hollered loudly at Dave," says Becky. Dave ran out to find his son quite agitated. "I tried to get you too look," said Jordan. "There was a girl standing beside me and now she's gone." But he refused to repeat what he had seen to his mother. "He wouldn't talk about it," says Becky.

There were other occasions that Becky is sure Jordan saw the ghost, but he kept the details to himself. "There's an office upstairs with a couch and television, and every now and again Jordan would come down and wouldn't go back up," Becky says. "I would ask him if the ghost was messing with him again, and he would just say he could hear things."

Becky's experiences have been less definitive. "I haven't seen anything really solid, if you will. Lots of times I think someone has just walked through the restaurant, but no one is there." She is sure, however, that one night she did see someone walk through the dining room just after they had closed. The lights were turned off, and in the darkness she saw a figure "for about three seconds, and then it disappeared."

She also had a run-in with something that literally took her breath away. "I was up here one morning waiting on a delivery truck. I went to the washroom and left the door open because I knew I was alone, and that way I could hear the truck. As I was walking back out, it felt like I ran into somebody." The impact left Becky breathless. "I felt it. But there was nothing there." She went on to say, "It's not frightening. You never feel like anything will harm you. It's a goose-bumpy thing."

The paranormal researchers and the Haddens agree that there might be more than one supernatural presence at the Greenbrier. Friends of the family claim they saw Dave's father, Dean, in the restaurant several days after he died. They were in the bar and heard a noise. When they turned to look, they briefly saw Dean still wearing his chef's attire and smiling broadly. Becky is sure alcohol was involved, but says, "I am also sure they had not consumed enough to be hallucinating."

And the Haddens aren't sure, but they feel that former owner Blanche Moffat may have paid them a ghostly visit recently. The incident happened to be captured on a digital camera by an enthusiastic tourist.

A lot of people take pictures in hopes of netting proof of the paranormal entities. Most people go home with nice pictures of the Greenbrier's interior, but one man had the encounter of a lifetime. "He got some of the best pictures I have ever seen," enthuses Becky. The man walked upstairs to an area used as a private dining room, taking pictures as he went. Becky recalls that the lights were off and the fellow's wife was behind him. "As he got to top of the stairs he kept snapping pictures, and then in his camera's display screen he saw the face and hair of an old woman. The actual facial part wasn't clear, but the outline was so clear he jumped and almost knocked his wife down the stairs." The man rushed down to show Becky, and when he scrolled through his images, the sight of the strange ghostly outline caused him to start again.

The man also took two consecutive pictures in the lobby that show a three-foot blur, "a big ball of light moving. There is no way they could have been altered because I saw them right after he took them," Becky declares. "I just wish he would send me copies because they really were the best photos anyone has taken."

That incident happened in September 2008, and Becky says the strange thing is that Dave read in a paper that it was the 31st anniversary of Blanche Moffat's death that day. "The picture looked like an older woman, so it just struck us as odd."

Most of the time, the Greenbrier is just a relaxing, out-of-the-way place to have a delicious meal surrounded by rustic elegance. But every now and then, there is something extra on the menu. "It's kind of random," says Becky. "We will go a couple of months and not see anything. It's very unpredictable." So if you happen to be driving on Highway 321 near Gatlinburg, drop by. You may catch a glimpse of Lydia, and at the very least you will get a unique dining experience.

Barley's Taproom

Asheville, North Carolina

There are all the usual jokes about bars being "spirited" places, and most of the stories have nothing to do with ghosts. Then there is Barley's Taproom in the arts and entertainment district of Asheville, North Carolina. The 8000-square-foot space houses a restaurant and stage on the site of the city's largest mass murder. So can you really be surprised to hear that the staff encounter eerie entities while serving the patrons?

Original owner Jimi Rentz did not know his establishment had a dodgy history when he and his former business partner Doug Beatty bought the building in September 1994. By then it was a television repair shop, and people thought of it as a restored 1920s appliance store. It became clear early on that something strange lurked in the old building.

One of the first people to get a taste of the paranormal was a contractor from South Carolina who had been hired to work on the pine flooring. He was brought in to cut the floor boards, which is a two-step process. "You cut them across the grain first," explains Jimi. "Then you cut them with the grain. This old guy from Greenville had finished the cross cut when the elevator came up by itself and the door opened." Interesting but hardly spooky, you may think. Except for this: "We have an old elevator in the building," says Jimi. "Fully manual. You know the kind, where you have to close the door, then close the cage, then push the button to make it go." There was no one in the elevator. It was operating itself. The workman quit without finishing, leaving the wood half cut— he even ran out without his tools.

"We had a cleaning lady who worked here from the time we opened in 1994 until around 1997," recalls Jimi. "She swore up and down that we had a portal in the second floor ceiling and that she could feel spirits coming through it and into the building."

One of the servers, a young woman named Cynthia, saw an apparition while on duty one night. On this particular evening there was no band scheduled to perform, so tables had been set out on the stage area. That's where Cynthia was working when she saw a female figure walk up the stairs to the second floor and disappear. "She was a nice preacher's daughter," says Jimi. "She kind of freaked out. And then one of the customers asked her, 'Did you see that?' And that really got her." Cynthia no longer works at Barley's Taproom.

Kara Tebaldi worked at Barley's for 10 years. During most of that time she did not see anything that might be considered paranormal, but often when closing up late at night, she says, "I would have sensations or feelings that something was around." Kara had heard the rumors about Barley's ghosts, but she had never taken them seriously. "It can get a bit eerie though, just the unknown. I guess on some level I am a believer, but you still feel weird when it happens to you." So she would say out loud, "Okay, I know you're here. I'm just finishing up and then you can have your space."

Kara did have an encounter a few years ago that changed the ghost's status from rumor to reality for her. "It was after hours, and I was enjoying a beer with some of my coworkers. There were only two women in the group," she recounts. "I went to the bathroom, and while in the stall I heard someone come in. Since there was only one other woman in our group I figured it was her, so I continued my conversation. But when I came out the room was absolutely empty. I went out and asked if she had come in; she said no." Rather than being scared, Kara says she feels lucky that she got to have the experience. "I never really mentioned it until a couple of years later, when another coworker shared that she had seen the figure of a woman in the bathroom. Then I knew for sure my mind wasn't playing tricks on me."

Former owner Doug Beatty reportedly heard footsteps upstairs when there was no one there. He also shared with others an unusual sighting—that of a figure passing quickly by a second-floor window. It was strange because there is no walkway or anything on which someone could stand.

Who might the ghosts be? It's hard to say. Jimi asked around, and an old-timer told him that the area used to be a rather rough "Bowery-style" district, and that there may have been a hotel on the site with some questionable clientele. In addition, blood stained the streets in November 1906 after a fugitive named Will Harris shot his way up the street, killing five people, including two police officers, and injuring many more before dying in a hail of bullets. It is reported that a posse of more than a thousand men tracked him down and let loose with more than a hundred bullets fired into Harris' body to put an end to the largest killing spree in Asheville history. And if that is not enough, right behind Barley's is the site of the old public gallows where criminals met their death for many years.

Barley's Taproom is now featured on two ghost tours. As well, paranormal investigators love to come, take pictures, record sounds and try to assess where the activity originates and what the source of the hauntings might be. So far the findings suggest the presence of paranormal energies, but there is nothing to draw any definitive conclusions.

For Jimi, an unsolicited photograph taken on March 9, 2008, by a visitor from Florida represents the best evidence to date that they have ghosts. The woman sent the photo by email. "The picture is that of a little ghost girl," says Jimi. "The woman was leaving and turned around to take a picture of our front doors. When she got home, she saw this little girl in a period coat and appearing to have something like braces or a mandible in her mouth. She is standing, but her legs seem to be between the panes of glass of the inner door."

For his part, Jimi hangs around hoping to catch a glimpse of one of the not-so-regular regulars. "I give them every chance I can to talk to me or show me something," he says.

"We have a collection of 200 tap handles, and I will say, 'You can turn them a little, show me you're here,' but they never do."

So if in Asheville, get in line to see the ghosts at Barley's. Sign up for a ghost tour, or just stop by for a brew and keep your eyes open.

The Library Club Restaurant
Sapphire Valley, North Carolina

Nestled in the southern crest of the Blue Ridge Mountains, Sapphire Valley's Library Club Restaurant sits peacefully surrounded by emerald forests, spectacular waterfalls and mountains that rise to 5000 feet. Despite the bucolic setting, boring is never on the menu of this historic eatery.

Pots of boiling water fly off the stove when no one is near. Gas burners on the stove self-ignite and send flames shooting nearly a foot high. Books fly off shelves. Patrons get the occasional nudge. "Nothing bad," says owner Megan Miller. "More playful." Then there is the virtual family of phantoms—a man, a woman and a little girl—seen quite often on or near the main staircase.

Megan and her husband Mark bought the club in 2006 knowing it was haunted. "We have been members since 1999. Sapphire Valley is a dry community, part of Southern Jackson County, which prohibits the sale of alcohol at restaurants and stores," explains Megan. "But you can serve alcohol in private, members-only clubs. And when we would come to have dinner, we would hear stories from the staff about the odd things they had seen."

The tales didn't dampen Megan and Mark's enthusiasm for buying the Library Club when the opportunity presented itself. "It has an interesting story even without the ghosts," Megan tells me. The building has been part of community history for almost 150 years. Built in 1864, it was part of a working farm that provided vegetables, fruit, meat and dairy products to the old Fairfield Inn, about half a mile away. The Library took its name from the lounge in the Fairfield Inn. In 1992, it was established as a private dining club. Previous owners undertook major renovations and expansion to the facility in 1999, but the original structure maintains its architectural integrity—and a few ghosts.

It's hard to say how far back the stories of strange happenings go. Some members of the staff have worked at the Library Club for many years, and it's been a part of their work experience from the beginning. After five years serving up drinks, bartender Ken says he has seen enough that he no longer gets "as rattled by it as before. I try not to let my imagination run away, and I'm not a big believer," he tells me. "At least, I wasn't until I started working here. And I don't drink while I'm working, so I know what I saw."

What changed Ken's nonbeliever status? First he saw a little girl wearing a white nightgown or dress standing near the doorway at the foot of the stairs that lead to the upstairs offices. "You see things out of the corner of your eye a lot here, but this was different," he explains. "I watched a little girl in an old-time flowing nightdress come down the steps in the old part of the house, go across the hallway and disappear into the wall."

Then Ken was the brunt of what might have been a super-natural prank. One night when he was closing up, he pushed all the bar stools up against the bar as part of his routine clean up and then went upstairs to the office to finish closing out. "I'm kind of anal retentive when I have to do clean up. I like things to be done right. And when I go upstairs to open the safe and count the money, I always lock myself in so I know that no one can get in." You can imagine his surprise when he came back down to go home and saw that every other bar stool was pulled out and turned around facing away from the bar. "I didn't hear any sounds either. You'd think you'd hear furniture being moved."

Perhaps the incident that put it over the top for Ken happened one night as he worked in the office (in the old part of the house). As he tallied the day's cash, a couple of papers fell off a bookshelf. "I said, 'Okay, I know you're here.' But I guess I didn't pay enough attention," says Ken, "because then the papers really started flying." As sheets of paper fell to the floor, Ken packed up and left. "I came back the next day to finish my work."

Kim Van Coppenole saw nothing of the Library Club's ghostly entities in her five years working as a server, but just a few weeks into bartending she discovered what all the talk was about. "As a bartender you close the place up, so you're by yourself. I didn't want to see anything so I would hurry to close, and I would talk out loud, saying to whatever might be listening, 'Don't come out, I don't want to see you.' But I finally got comfortable and forgot." While mopping and sweeping, Kim distinctly saw a little girl wearing a dress go down the hallway. "Instead of being scared," she says, "I got mad. I said, 'What are you doing? I told you not to come out.'"

Now, after two years working behind the bar, Kim has a litany of experiences with whatever it is that inhabits her workplace. "I believe there is more than one," she says. There are the little things: a coffee pot swishing as if just placed down when no one is around, seeing shadows from the corner of her eye, hearing footsteps, televisions turning on by themselves and a general feeling that someone is watching. Kim looks for a scientific explanation for things until there is no way to rationally explain them; she feels it is too easy to blame unusual events on a ghost. So that leads to the other not-so-little experiences in her growing catalogue of "things you don't see every day and can't explain."

One night Kim went back into the kitchen after a cigarette break. As she opened the back door she saw the reflection of a man and thought it must be someone in the parking lot. However, as she stood there and looked around, there was no one outside. "Then I realized there was no glass in the door, just a screen. So I didn't see a reflection, I saw an apparition." Much like a reflection, though, the man's image was indistinct. "He was tall, had broad shoulders, but I couldn't make out his face," she recalls.

Kim once watched as a full drink tipped over without anyone near. "I tried to recreate it," she says, "because I was looking for any plausible explanation, but I just couldn't do it." She also had the feeling of having someone put a hand on her hip, and though she would like to think it was just her shirt coming untucked, "it felt very much like a hand."

The upstairs office where staff members go to complete paperwork after the Library Club closes is a place in which Kim would rather not dally. "I often see shadows out of the corner of my eye. It's very creepy and once you close up, you never go back upstairs." One night Kim forgot her cell phone in the office and had to return to retrieve it. As she entered the office a large stack of magazines fell over. "I try to explain it naturally—maybe my step was heavy enough to cause them to fall," she says. "Except that then I heard Ken had a similar experience. So it's hard to know what to think."

Most recently, Kim saw a "huge black shadow go down the hallway." It was a Sunday, and she was alone. She remembered too late to admonish the spirits not to come out. "I usually tell them I'm not comfortable with this, but I forgot."

Despite the scary moments, most of the employees say that whatever they keep encountering is not malicious— more playful than anything—and doesn't have them looking for work elsewhere. However, in the kitchen, which is believed to be in the same place as it was in the original house, there have been a few instances that have made Megan pause—though she still feels the presence is benign. "Our sous-chef was in the kitchen alone and went into a different part of the kitchen in search of something. There was a loud bang, and when he returned he saw a large pot of boiling water on the floor." On three separate occasions, employees have come into the kitchen in the morning— before anyone had been in to work—to find flames shooting a foot high from one of the burners on the stove, but the chef would swear everything had been properly shut down the night before. And the pastry chef reported hearing the radio turn on by itself more than once.

The club's warm, friendly atmosphere draws in a large portion of the local business crowd, and according to Megan, "our regulars have seen a lot." Sue Bumgarner, the director of the Chamber of Commerce, had her first encounter on her first visit to the Library Club back in the early 1990s. She was sitting at the bar when she felt something rub her leg. "I was there with my daughter and I thought perhaps she wanted my attention, but she was busy talking to someone else." Then it happened again. Her daughter denied touching her. Shocked by the sensation, Sue got up and went outside to the patio. After a time, she came back in and sat down again, only to be accosted once more. "I felt someone put their arm firmly around my shoulder and pull me over to one side," she recalls. "The person I was talking to asked me if I was all right, and I replied, 'No!'" And just as Sue registered that something was touching her, one of the books flew off the shelf behind her and landed on the floor. She left feeling quite unnerved.

A couple of weeks later, Sue returned. This time the spirit got a little too friendly. "I felt like I was being crowded," she says, "like I was constantly being nudged. It continued for about half an hour, so then I said, 'Just give me my tab and I will never be back here again.' The bartender laughed and said, 'Oh, is it the ghost again?'" Sue wasn't amused.

Eventually the Library Club's welcoming environment drew her back, but Sue says the experience changed her. "I didn't believe in ghosts before, but now I do. When something like that happens to you, you realize there is more around than what meets the eye." She also wonders if it might be a family member trying to get in touch, because it turns out that relatives on her grandmother's side—the Monteiths— used to live in the house many years ago. "When I go there, I still look around and wonder if I will see something."

The tally of unusual events continues to rise. Ken and another bartender named Chip say that on several occasions they have seen shadows moving near the hall by the bathrooms. A three-year-old girl visiting with her family kept talking about a man she saw when no one else saw anyone.

Megan's husband Mark is often in the Library Club alone, arriving very early before any of the other employees. "When you're alone, it's a different experience," says Megan. While upstairs in the office Mark hears sounds as if someone is rattling around downstairs, but when he investigates there is never anyone visible. According to Megan, he also sees the figure of a woman out of the corner of his eye—an older woman in a white dress, with her hair pinned up. Although he has seen the woman quite often, Mark has not been close enough to identify her.

There have only been three owners of the property, though dozens of tenants have lived in the house. After years as a farm, it eventually became an antique store. Megan salvaged dozens of photographs of previous residents, but so far no one has been able to point a finger at one of the faces to give a name to the ghosts. She is particularly interested in the child ghost that plays around and under the stairs. "I have asked locals here if a child ever died in the house, but no one seems to know."

In May 2008, there was an unexpected opportunity for Megan to learn more about the spirits in her club. Sprout Dvorak and Scott Walker arrived for a holiday, but the ghost trackers immediately sensed the presence of paranormal activity. Sprout, who is an investigator with the Peace River Ghost Trackers, was prompted by her intuition to ask Megan about the restaurant's ghost stories. Once she heard the tales, Sprout asked if she and her husband could do an impromptu investigation. "We didn't do a full investigation because we were on holiday and didn't have our proper equipment, but we set up our digital cameras, our audio recorders and our hi-8 video camera to see what we might capture on tape," says Sprout. Megan, Mark, Ken and Chip joined Sprout and Scott for the late-night investigation. Their report is available online, but the group had limited success. "We did not obtain any hard evidence on this investigation to be able to prove or disprove any of the claims of paranormal activity," reports Sprout. But they did have a couple of moments that made the duo decide to return for a follow-up session.

"At 1:25 AM we all witnessed the smell of soap at the doorway to the bar," says Sprout. She tells me it was strong, old-fashioned smelling soap, and everyone could smell it distinctly. The smell wafted through the area to the hallway. In the report Sprout notes that the doorway is believed to be the original back door to the house and theorizes that the laundry may have been done in that area. Scott asked out loud for the smell to go away, and it did. When he asked for it to return, the smell returned. "We believe that we were communicating with an intelligent spirit, and we are grateful for the experience," says Sprout. The only other unusual readings occurred just a minute after the soap smell when their EMF meter registered a brief spike in front of the bar.

The Peace River Ghost Tracker team will return with all their equipment to perform a full investigation. "We are a meticulous group," says Sprout. "We work hard to disprove the paranormal before jumping to conclusions." But they feel sure there is more to the Library Club than meets the eye.

Megan is excited to have the team return. "I am intrigued," she says. "I have not seen anything, but I'm not really attuned to that sort of vibration. But I believe in the supernatural, and I believe there is something to the things people experience here."

The Baker Peters Jazz Club

Knoxville, Tennessee

With its plush interior, warm intimate spaces and cool jazz, the posh Baker Peters Jazz Club is all about atmosphere. And nothing charges an atmosphere more than the tantalizing possibility of encountering a ghost. "It's definitely a huge part of our business," says manager Jason Holt. "People want to see the door with the bullet holes and hear about Abner."

The history of this two-story, 1840s home-turned-lounge is as rich as the meals dished out by the chef. You take one Confederate sympathizer, mix in a shoot-out with Union soldiers and then add a vengeful son to create one explosive tale.

Most of the ghostly activity dates back to June 19, 1863. Up to that point in the Civil War, Dr. James Harvey Baker had tended wounded Confederate soldiers in his home on the corner of Kingston Pike and Baker's Creek. When he heard that the Union army may be dropping by, he met the scouting party on his porch armed with a Colt pistol and a Maynard rifle. Despite his claim that the soldiers should not shoot because he was a private citizen, a short gun fight ensued. Dr. Baker dodged the bullets and ran inside while the soldiers surrounded the house. Neighbor James Parl told the Knoxville *Daily Register* that Dr. Baker told his wife it was too late to escape and to take the children upstairs. The entire family, along with slaves, crowded into one of the bedrooms while soldiers stormed into the building.

Mrs. Baker pleaded for her family's life on the second-floor landing, according to Mr. Parl's statement on July 22, but she came close to being shot herself. Bullets ripped through the bedroom door just seconds after Mrs. Baker returned to the room to comfort her children. Dr. Baker "threw the door wide open and discharged the two remaining balls in his pistol," unleashing a hail of ammunition from the Union army. Two bullets found their mark, and the doctor told his wife, "Agnes, I am killed."

Son Abner, who fought for the Confederates, returned home to find the house ransacked and his father dead. At this point, history becomes somewhat blurred. By most accounts, Abner vowed revenge on the informant who told the Union army about his father harboring Confederate soldiers. In one version he followed through and killed Knoxville's postmaster, William Hall. In retaliation, some of Hall's friends ambushed Abner and either hanged him from a tree or dragged him behind a horse until he was dead. Another version has it that Abner got into a fight with William Hall on the steps to the courthouse and was subsequently lynched by the crowd. Or there is the story that he went to jail but was dragged from his cell and hanged by a mob on September 4, 1865. However it happened, Abner met an unpleasant end like his father, and neither of them left the house they fought so hard to protect.

The brick house now belongs to a dentist (his office is on the first floor), and several other restaurants occupied the second floor prior to it becoming the Baker Peters Jazz Club. The house was remodeled, and the door with the bullet holes is now the first-floor entryway to the dental office. Staff of the club will be happy to point it out, along with a photo taken in the lobby before it was a jazz club that shows that the ghosts have been around for some time. The blurred image shows a face in a window—it is thought to be Abner's reflection caught in the glass—and another image of a figure in the empty dining room.

"I have been here nine or 10 months and was told the basic story when I started. I'm here by myself a lot at night and haven't witnessed anything firsthand," says Jason. "But I typically have to respond a few times a month to the alarm going off in the middle of the night for no reason." Then he explains that there actually *is* a reason, but it generates more questions than answers. "The motion detector will be set off by pots and pans falling on the floor in the kitchen or glasses being knocked over in the dining room. It's an old house, things shift, but realistically, who knows? I try to find a reason for things, more for peace of mind for the staff, but it's hard to explain."

A former assistant manager named Bob Wilson told the *Knoxville News Sentinel* on October 30, 2005, that he had an unnerving experience one day in 2002. Wilson heard his name coming from a computer at which he worked. "A man's voice says, 'Robert, Robert.' We don't have a sound chip in our computer."

There are also stories of a yellow light that drifts from room to room, and some employees have heard footsteps.

Over the years, several groups with an interest in seeking out the paranormal have come to the house in hopes of meeting the Baker ghosts. In fact, many groups that investigate the house say that Abner is the least obvious presence among the bevy of entities they encounter. "Abner is the ghost we are most known for," says Jason, "but what is eerie to me is that every one of these groups independently found other ghosts, and they all found the same ones." Among the other spirits that ghost hunters claim to meet are a middle-aged woman thought to be a slave who took care of the house or the children, and a young girl whose spirit is often found on the stairs. "That always sends a chill up my spine," admits Jason, who adds that he may need to start taking "the ghost thing" a little more seriously.

Ghost hunters from the Alternate Realities Center spent a night in October 2005 tracking down the spirits after the bar had closed and all the patrons were gone. The team took dozens of pictures of orbs, which many sceptics dismiss as dust flecks or light flares. But the group also took a digital photograph that shows the head and chest of a man wearing 19th-century clothing reflected in a second-floor window. Using copper divining (or dowsing) rods, the team located four spirits on the upper floor: two male and two female. During the "conversation," one spirit was identified as Abner Baker. Another spirit was that of a female servant.

A long term investigation that began in earnest in fall 2008 by Spirit Hunters of Knoxville (SHOK) turned up some even more startling information. According to SHOK's founder, Andrea Jamison, there are more than half a dozen intelligent spirits in the house, and she claims that she and her team "talk to Dr. Baker all the time."

Using a machine they call a "ghost box," Andrea says that they have real-time conversations with the home's original owner and with some of the other ghosts that reside there. She describes the equipment they use as looking like a "huge iPod" and says that the machine continuously scans the frequencies, which allows the spirit to speak through different channels, and that they can hear what is said either through headphones or a speaker. So why doesn't every ghost hunting group use one? "It's still an iffy piece of equipment," admits

Andrea, "but it works, and I can tell you where Dr. Baker sits in the house. I take my equipment to the space and he sets it off every time. Now he is used to me and asks me to come over. You can tell when you are talking to him because he uses words from his time like 'fandangled.'"

Dr. Baker is aware he is dead, says Andrea, but he stays to watch over his home, "and he doesn't want anyone to forget him. He's a peaceful spirit. He's not crazy about his home being a jazz club, but as long as they respect it, he's okay with it." The dead doctor told the SHOK team that he doesn't talk to other investigative teams because he feels they do not respect him.

Apparently the doctor's sense of humor survived his death. Andrea noticed one day that on the other side of the door with the bullet holes something would block the light, then allow the light through. It happened a few times, so she looked through the hole but couldn't see anything. "The door was locked because it goes to the dental office, which was closed, so I couldn't open it to see what was on the other side. Instead I put my camera up to the hole and took a picture. I was stunned to see a blue eyeball looking back at me." Andrea found out in a later conversation with Dr. Baker that he did it as a joke, and he apologized. "He said, 'I scared you, I'm sorry.' But he laughed."

Who else is in the home? SHOK's investigators confirmed that Abner remains in the house, "but he doesn't talk much and keeps to himself." Then there is nine-year-old Amy, Dr. Baker's niece who fell down the stairs after she tripped while chasing a ball. She died from the fall. "I cried when I heard the story," says Andrea, "but Dr. Baker said, 'Don't cry, she's at peace.'" The pots and glasses that fall are Amy's handiwork because she gets bored. But when asked why she will not move on, the little girl says that she prefers to stay with her uncle.

"We have encountered Jeb. He was either a slave or a hired hand around the house," lists Andrea, going through the other ghosts. "He worked in the kitchen for Dr. Baker and is a strong presence there. He can't move on because Anne will not allow him to. He was supposed to be watching Amy the day she fell, and Anne is still angry." Anne is another spirit in the house, either Amy's mother or aunt.

Then there is Grace, a maid or slave who worked for the Bakers. She is a quiet spirit that doesn't say much. And there is a Cuban spirit that the SHOK team calls "Rifleman McGuire." The story is that his son was being treated for the flu by Dr. Baker, so he came back to be with his son. The boy died in the house, and for some reason the father's spirit hangs around. "He must think his son's spirit is there," says Andrea. SHOK discovered the unusual presence in a picture they took that can be seen on their website. In the picture you can see one of the investigators reflected in a window, and you can see the Cuban man sitting next to her.

The team's other noteworthy photo is one that caught a full body apparition. It too is on SHOK's website. "It was our first time at the house, and 4500 pictures later, I caught that one," says Andrea. "Nobody knew who it was. There are no pictures of Dr. Baker, so no one could say if it was him. But he is wearing 1920s clothing. Then one of the managers found a pile of photos from the 1900s and I saw one that matched. On the back it identified the man as Robert Peters." Mr. Peters was the second owner of the home.

There may be other spirits yet to come forward and chat with the SHOK team. There was an incident recently where the whole team plus restaurant employees were upstairs when the motion sensors on the main floor went off, "for no reason," declares Andrea.

And so it goes. Old buildings with creaky floors easily wear the mantle of being haunted, but in the case of this antebellum house, perhaps there is cause for the label. You can visit and decide for yourself.

The Bijou Theatre

Knoxville, Tennessee

The Bijou Theatre in Knoxville, Tennessee, is the fourth oldest building in the city, and it has an impressive, if somewhat seedy, history. It has survived wars and fires. It has undergone more than a dozen name changes, structural changes and business changes. It has been an apartment building, a tavern, a hospital, a used car lot and fruit stand, a burlesque dance hall, a whorehouse, an X-rated movie house and a hotel/theater. It has hosted artists from the Marx Brothers to Dizzy Gillespie to Sheryl Crow. And this refurbished "gem of the south" can add one more noteworthy distinction to the list: it is haunted—really, really haunted.

The Bijou was built in 1817 as the Lamar House and did not become a theater until 1908. It operated as the principal house for the Knoxville Opera and Symphony. During the Civil War the Bijou was transformed into a hospital. During the siege in which General Ambrose Burnside took Knoxville for the Union, a Union colonel named William Sanders was brought to the Bijou to be treated for his injuries. He died there the next day, and his ghost is one of the main entities said to roam the present-day theater.

A century later, during the 1960s, the theater became known as the Bijou Art Theatre, which was a nice way of saying it ran adult-only, X-rated movies. The Lamar House attached to the back of the theater had a reputation for even more sexually explicit entertainment. Prostitution proliferated. The Bijou entered its darkest days.

The building had changed hands a few times, and somehow the elderly woman who owned it during this time did not realize what enterprise ran within the deteriorating and increasingly dingy walls. Upon her death the building passed to a church, which leased it to a man who ran a burlesque parlor. The theater closed in 1973 for unpaid taxes and rent.

Slated for demolition, it got a reprieve in 1975 by being added to the list of historical places in Knoxville. An intense fundraising campaign brought the theater back from the brink, though it teetered again in 2005 when owners defaulted on the mortgage. This virtual phoenix of a theater was salvaged by two local businessmen, and after a massive refurbishing, the theater reopened in June 2006.

Through all the upheaval, the ghosts remained. The origins of the majority of the entities that haunt the Bijou Theatre have not been determined, though there is consensus that one of the spirits is that of the dead colonel, William Sanders. He apparently died in the bridal suite of the Lamar House. When that part was torn down, the colonel's ghost migrated to the theater.

Other ghosts said to haunt the place are well-known actors who graced the stage, such as Al Jolson. There is the spirit of a stagehand known as Smiley who apparently fell from the ceiling in the early 20th century and died. Phantom prostitutes are also said to inhabit the area.

The ghosts make their presence known by making noises. People hear sighs, and some people have been touched by invisible hands. Sometimes apparitions are seen floating in the theater or on the stage, especially if no one else is around. These ghosts are said to be generally happy and harmless. "There is no doubt about it that it's haunted," says assistant manager Jeanine Brown of the theater. "I believe in all this, although I'm here by myself a lot and haven't experienced anything."

Bijou's technical director, Jason Fogerty, told the *Knoxville News Sentinel* in January 2009, "I saw a ghost walk out from behind a curtain. It was at the end of a 70-hour week, so I'm not quite sure if it was my mind playing tricks on me. But I stuck my head out through the stage and saw somebody walk out from behind a curtain. It was probably about four or five seconds, kind of see-through, dressed in old clothes. It was a man." Could it have been a vaudevillian trying to get in another bow? Or was it the colonel wandering about?

Even if the spirits are benign, one actress named Laura must, as she says, "screw up my courage and turn on every possible light just to step into the place alone anymore." During rehearsals for a play Laura was in, she repeatedly saw figures out of the corner of her eye in the balconies, particularly at the center of the first balcony.

The ghost of a little girl haunts the theater. No one knows who she is, but she has been heard singing on the stage when only one or two people are around. One story is that a box office worker was locking up at the end of the day and found a girl standing inside the theater. She asked the girl who she was and why she was there but did not get any answer. The employee told the girl to come out into the lobby with her and walked out, but turned around to find the girl had disappeared.

A former director standing in the lobby heard someone walking down the stairs from the balcony. He looked up to see who it was, and as the footsteps reached the point where he should have been able to see the person, the steps continued—but no person appeared.

After two investigations conducted by the East Tennessee Paranormal Research Society (ETPRS) in 2003 and 2006, the group has a myriad of photos of apparitions, orbs, shadow ghosts and ectoplasm, not to mention video of an actual ghost. They also recorded dozens of electronic voice phenomena (EVPs) throughout the building, from the basement and first-floor auditorium and stage to the fourth floor, where the old hotel used to be.

Tracy Franklin, president of the ETPRS, directed me to his society's website for evidence gathered on July 21, 2006, of the spirits that waft about the 1500-seat theater. Photographs of orbs were taken in several rooms, including the fourth-floor room where the colonel died. The ETPRS site explains, "These pics [sic] of the orbs are unique. These orbs showed up either after a question was asked or after an appearance of a shadow. Orbs are the hardest paranormal evidence to prove, but again we think that these are important because of the situation. No orb was present until a question was asked."

Investigators took many pictures on the first balcony and in the second-floor restroom of what they call "Type B shadow ghosts." The following is posted next to the pictures: "There is a theory that a spirit's natural form is an orb. That a shadow ghost must return to the orb form before moving quickly out of an area. If this is true then it might be expected if a flash picture is taken, and startles it, or causes it to want to leave, it will have to return to an orb first. The thing about this is that after each picture that captured a shadow ghost another picture was taken right after. And in each after shot there was an orb present where the shadow ghost was."

Another photograph taken in the theater shows what they believe is a ghost child standing in the aisle. "You can see the head, the ear and the hair, and if you look carefully you can even see some eyes looking at you," says Sean Dudley, an ETPRS investigator. He says this photo is not a case of the camera lying.

The old hotel area on the fourth floor sits empty, not yet remodeled. It looks exactly the same as it did decades ago. Up there, EVPs sound as if they understand what investigators were saying. In one, in which Tracy Franklin suggests the spirits can be provoked, a sarcastic "Really?" can be heard. And perhaps residual energy from the days when prostitutes worked there lingers on, as one male voice says, "This time let's take a shower," and a female voice responds, "The shower's cold."

The best evidence, according to the ETPRS team, is a short video taken in a second-floor washroom of what they claim is an apparition—"100% authentic video of a real ghost"—that was captured in infrared. The video recorded by Sean Dudley is believed to corroborate the experience of an employee who was trapped in a stall in the ladies' room by some paranormal entity. The door to her stall refused to open, and when she finally crawled out under the door there was no one else in the room.

The explanation of the video says, "The investigator is standing in the only doorway to the stalls. Only walls are to either side of the stalls. The investigator pans across the whole bathroom, the stalls and then pans behind himself. When the investigator pans back to the stalls an apparition appears from the bottom of the camera and takes off to the camera-man's left. As you see in the video the apparition starts to change shape and starts to dissipate toward a wall. The apparition appears at the same stall that the patron was locked in."

In watching the video, you can definitely see something skirt through the bottom left corner of the screen. "Seems to be a ghost to me," says Sean Dudley. "It has eyes, looks right at you as soon as it comes into frame and then darts away and changes form at the last second. I feel quite confident that I captured a ghost on video." Although there is no way to verify for sure what was captured on tape, it is definitely something hard to explain.

During the March 2003 ghost hunt, the team experienced cold spots and heard sounds like coins dropping, knocking and a vacuum cleaner when no one was present to make the sounds. But at 3:30 AM, one of the investigators got an unexpected bunkmate in the lobby. The report states that there was "an icy cold finger poking a remaining investigator in the side. She tried to ignore it and said aloud that she needed to get some sleep. Minutes later she felt the blanket beside her being pushed down and turned her head enough to witness the pillow beside her head pressing down slowly." It appears that even ghosts like to snuggle.

What to make of all this? If you hear something unusual, maybe it's just a centuries-old building creaking and settling. But don't be surprised to hear laughter or see movements from the corner of your eye. It might be a Civil War colonel or even a "working girl" visiting from beyond the grave.

The Barter Theatre

Abingdon, Virginia

Through adversity comes greatness, and the Appalachian town of Abingdon received one of its prized possessions out of the challenges wrought by the Great Depression. The Barter Theatre was born at a time when money was scarce but a sack of potatoes could get you a seat at a show. And to this day, the ghost of the man who came up with the idea of exchanging ham for Hamlet still oversees his treasured stage.

It was the 1930s, and making a living as an actor took gumption. In the hardship of the depression, people did not have money to spare to support local theaters. Unemployed and struggling to survive but undeterred, Virginian actor Robert Porterfield moved to Abingdon with a group of fellow thespians, and they took over an old Presbyterian church to set up their theater company.

Because most people could not afford the ticket price of 40 cents, Porterfield proposed an unorthodox idea to the cast.

They agreed, and on June 10, 1933, the Barter Theatre opened with the proclamation, "With vegetables you cannot sell, you can buy a good laugh." By accepting the equivalent of the ticket price in produce, Porterfield created an opportunity for anyone in the community to attend. The notion was the surprise hit of the season. The first shows were "sell-outs," with four out of five people handing over dairy products, vegetables and even livestock. The squawking chickens were a little distracting for the actors, but in the end, bartering to hear the bard worked. The cast may not have earned enough to retire, but everyone gained weight!

An impassioned Porterfield scrounged, borrowed and recycled to give theater-goers a performance center that would inspire them to attend. He carted away $75,000 worth of seats, paintings, art and carpeting from New York City's Empire Theatre prior to its destruction. Porterfield also hauled away the Empire's entire lighting system, designed and installed by inventor Thomas Edison, and lit the Barter Theatre with it until the mid-1970s.

Porterfield's theater provided a start for many marquee names, including Ernest Borgnine, Gregory Peck and Ned Beatty. It also attracted praise from President John F. Kennedy. Today the Barter Theatre holds the honor of being the State Theater of Virginia. After investing so much of himself in the Barter, it is small wonder that Robert Porterfield felt reluctant to leave it even after his death in 1971.

Courtney Bledsoe, the theater's associate director of marketing, says the main story is that actors would see Porterfield in the balcony pacing throughout a performance, particularly when the curtain rose on a new show. "On the opening nights actors would see a person walking around up there in a white suit," says Courtney. "Robert was known for really dressing up for opening night. After the show, new actors would say, 'Who was that guy walking around in the balcony the whole time?'"

The nattily dressed apparition has also been seen hanging around the box office and by his old office, but there haven't been many sightings since the mid-1990s. "Richard Rose became the artistic director in 1992, and he did a lot of renovations to the theater," explains Courtney. "When it was done, Richard took down this huge portrait of Robert Porterfield that hung in the lobby and went around to every area with it to see if he approved. From that time, no one has really seen Robert."

There are other spirits lurking about backstage and below in the theater's boiler room—and not all of them are as peaceful and friendly as the former founder. Actor Ned Beatty claimed to have been chased out of one of the dressing rooms by a mysterious dark shadow figure that came after him one night as he was leaving after a show.

Different teams of paranormal researchers have hunted through the theater to try to determine who that spirit might be. There is a theory that it is the disgruntled spirit of an actor who was fired by Porterfield. One investigation by a group called Tri-Cities Paranormal Research caught a disembodied voice on tape ordering them to leave—*now*. The team also suffered several equipment malfunctions and repeated draining of batteries, but nothing definitive could be concluded from the gathered evidence. The Tri-Cities Paranormal Research team says of its investigation, "We believe the Barter Theatre to have paranormal activity; however, we do not believe there is sufficient evidence for it to be labeled haunted."

The other ghost connected to the theater is what Courtney calls "the tunnel ghost." Every new employee gets the same tour that guests are given, and it includes a trip down to the tunnel that used to connect the Martha Washington Inn across the street (see page 66) to the building that the Barter Theatre now inhabits. "The story I was told is that the tunnel was used during the war when this was a town hall, and it was used to sneak weapons and ammunition out of the Martha," says Courtney. The Union Army found out about the tunnel and sent soldiers in from both sides, killing two soldiers.

"For years, the two happily haunted the tunnel. At our end in the boiler room, people felt things. In 1990, Main Street was widened and the tunnel collapsed, and then they unhappily haunted the area. The activity really picked up for about 10 years. Even now a lot of our crew won't work down there at night if they are alone," Courtney says. In her three years working at the Barter she has been down in the boiler room area quite a bit giving tours to people, and though she has "never felt anything," she admits it is a creepy room, and she doesn't linger long when she is there.

There is another—albeit unsubstantiated—story of a ghostly Civil War soldier that still wanders about the theater. The local lore suggests that if the soldier shows you his wounds, you will die within 48 hours. There is no record of it happening, so this might be one of those tales best saved for scaring the daylights out of people around a campfire.

It seems there are more ghosts—or at least unseen entities—in some of the other buildings associated with the theater. The company owns buildings on a former girls' school campus that they use for a variety of reasons: to house actors and staff, for rehearsals, for storing costumes and for making props. "One of our directors won't work in the rehearsal hall at night," Courtney says, "because of the creepy feeling you get and the noises that you hear." But there is a way to peacefully co-exist with whatever spirit shares the space. As you enter the building you must say out loud, "Okay, I'm just here to work and I won't harm this space." Then everything is fine. Otherwise, Courtney assures me, "the ghosts make it uneasy to be there."

Has Robert Porterfield been assured that his pride and joy is in good hands? Or does his spirit still hover like a mother hen behind a balcony pillar on opening night to watch the crowd's reaction? Perhaps Mr. Porterfield finally decided it was safe to slip away and leave the treading of the boards to those on this side of the veil.

4
Haunted Institutions

East Tennessee State University

Johnson City, Tennessee

Phantom founders, spectral suicide victims and a diligent (but deceased) librarian are among the massive cast of ghosts that populate East Tennessee State University. This Johnson City stronghold of education has been called the most haunted campus in the southern United States. There are certainly enough stories around to keep life interesting when textbooks just aren't stimulating enough.

Sidney Gilbreath, the university's founder and first president, is one of the ghosts said to keep watch over campus life. Gilbreath was a man of exacting standards, particularly for the female students enrolled at ETSU, and he may still pace about Gilbreath Hall worried about student conduct. His ghost is only experienced on the fourth floor of the hall, which is accessed through a janitor's closet. Janitors report more activity during a storm, but the ghost's actions are of a beneficent nature—closing windows and turning off lights. Locked doors will somehow become unlocked. There is also a report that one female student saw Gilbreath's figure standing in a window of the hall one evening. The Tri-Area Paranormal Research Group investigated and on the second floor of the hall found one measurable cold spot—thought to be an indicator of paranormal activity.

Within Burleson Hall is a haunted painting, inhabited by the spirit of former English professor Christine Burleson. The scholar taught at ETSU for four decades and was well-known for her love of all things Shakespeare. Burleson committed suicide in the 1970s after a debilitating disease left her wheelchair-bound and is now believed to haunt a painting of her father, David Sinclair Burleson, who was a charter member of the faculty during ETSU's early days. People claim that the eyes follow them in a most unsettling way as they move through the hall. The eyes, however, are not David's but Christine's. There have also been reports of hearing a woman moaning and of seeing the shadowy shape of a female apparition floating through the hallways. The Tri-Area Paranormal Research Group posted on its website a photograph of a shadow figure taken on the second floor—could it be an image of Christine Burleson's ghost?

At the Mathes Music Hall, *something* follows the maintenance workers around at night, but no one is sure just what that something is. Workers cleaning the building say that they hear footsteps following them, but the steps stop when they do. There is never anybody attached to the mysterious feet, but some ghost apparently likes to plod around after the dutiful cleaning staff. Many people report feeling cold spots in different parts of the hall. One worker claimed to hear crashing noises on the upper floor when she was alone in the building. Maybe the spirit is just lonely and looking for company; the Mathes Hall is known for its strange layout and the sense of isolation felt when entering the building.

One of ETSU's best-known ghost stories involves a building that was torn down in 1984. The screaming ghost of Cooper Hall was said to be Alice, the daughter of George Carter, the businessman who donated the land on which the university was built. Alice, the story goes, committed suicide by eating rat poison after her parents refused to let her marry the man of her choice. The grieving family had a stained glass window made in their daughter's image and installed it in the house, which later became a women's dormitory. Tales of otherworldly screams shattering the stillness late at night and of hearing a woman's voice singing were told for years. Even after the building was turned into a campus radio station and office space, people reported hearing strange noises. But George Carter didn't have a daughter—only a son names James Walter Carter. This crucial point was discovered by a local historian while researching the ghost stories. Photographs of James Carter show that he had long, blond hair, and it may be that he modeled for the stained glass artwork. So who might the spirit have been? Both the window and the building are long gone; it is now impossible to know.

Over at the Stafford Library, in the lower storage area known as "the old stacks," a former librarian is said to keep a close eye on her treasured books. Many students report feeling queasy in the library when they are hunting through the shelves and no one else is around. Others have even reported seeing a shadow figure moving briskly through the aisles.

At Yoakley Hall, which is now used for offices, there are stories of a very unhappy student ghost who committed suicide by jumping out of a top-floor window. Some people have spotted the figure of a woman leaning out from a third-floor window, and others say they see a person jump, but the figure disappears before hitting the ground. Perhaps the ghost regrets that last decision made in life.

Students living in the Lucille Clement dormitory told a reporter from the *East Tennessean* in October 2007 that their room is haunted. Bethany Eldrige and Hailey Wix claim that their ghost turns things on and off, and on one occasion it knocked over a plate of food. "I had a plate of lasagna on my bed ready to be eaten, and nothing was touching it, and the plate just flipped upside-down and hit the floor," Bethany told reporter Holly Blair.

Administrator Carol Fox sent along a list of reported hauntings that they put out for Halloween every year, and also inside Lucille Clement Hall is an energetic spirit known as "Marble Boy" for its habit of dumping what sounds like a bucket of marbles on an upper floor. Residents hear the racket, but when they make the trek upstairs to investigate, there is nothing there.

Over in the John P. Lamb Jr. Hall, mischievous spirits like to move objects around within locked offices and play with the elevators, making them move even when they appear empty.

Of course, the campus theaters will not be outdone in the ghost department. The architecturally beautiful Memorial Theatre on the grounds of the Veterans Affairs Medical Center is said to have ghosts in the half-basement below the stage. Performers in ETSU's student productions have noted that spirits seem to enjoy their dramatic performances. And in the Bud Frank Theatre in Gilbreath Hall, spectral spectators create an eerie dynamic for actors on stage. Many performers claim to have seen ghostly apparitions watching them during rehearsals.

Finally, the B. Carroll Reece Museum is said to be staked out by the noisy spirit of its namesake, Tennessee's first district congressman. The museum began in the late 1920s as a campus history project and over the years evolved into a "storehouse of knowledge." It also houses the ETSU Art Department's permanent collection of art. Reece died in 1961, and the museum was dedicated in his name four years later. Apparently the native Tennessean, buried in Johnson

City alongside his wife Louise, still likes to roam the museum at night, especially on the lower level.

So, although East Tennessee State University sees an influx of new faces every year and now boasts a student population of more than 13,000, it would seem that some campus dwellers like the idea of being a permanent part of the student body—even when they no longer possess a body of their own.

The Smith-McDowell House

Asheville, North Carolina

Several paranormal investigative teams can't be wrong. According to some of the top phantom probes, the historic Smith-McDowell House in Asheville, North Carolina, has ghosts—plenty of them. The ephemeral lady in white seen on the stairs, the little child and the feisty slave are just the ones they know about.

If the reports from the various teams of investigators are not enough to convince the most sceptical of minds, there are also the firsthand experiences of people such as Lisa Whitfield. She works at the house, now a heritage center, and says, "I didn't know anything of the house being haunted prior to coming here. I found out the first day I worked here and several people said they feel things or see things and I thought, oh Lord, where have I come?"

Where Lisa had come to work is cited as the "finest surviving example of brick antebellum architecture in western

North Carolina," according to the non-profit museum's website. The gorgeous four-story mansion was originally built using slave labor about 20 years before the Civil War on a plantation south of the nearby city of Asheville. At the time most homes were log cabins, so this massive brick edifice stood out as rare and impressive.

Colonel Daniel Smith had acquired the property through a land grant for soldiers of the Revolutionary War. His son James—said to be the first white child born west of the mountains in North Carolina—built the house around 1840 for his wife, Mary Patton. James died in 1856 as one of the richest and most influential men in North Carolina's history. His son John inherited the family home but died just one year later, so the house became the property of John's business partner, William Wallace McDowell. Through the Civil War, the house was an enclave for Confederate volunteers and was visited by Union troops.

When the war ended the McDowells suffered financially, and an era of changing ownership began. It belonged in succession to friends of the Vanderbilts, millionaire Brewster Chapman and businessman Herman Gudger. In 1951, the Catholic Church bought the property to turn it into a boy's school dormitory. In the mid-1970s, the now run-down building and grounds became the property of a local technical college, but the Western North Carolina Historical Association saved it in 1974 from almost certain destruction and restored it to its original glory, and it stands now as a heritage center and museum. With so many different families and all that goes with those various histories—illnesses, tragedies, deaths—it is not surprising that some energy lingers on to this day.

The notion of working alongside ghosts did not alarm Lisa Whitfield because the stories were relatively benign. She also thought nothing would happen to her—she does not consider herself to have the gift of sensitivity to the paranormal—but that view has changed. "Within the first few months of working here, I heard something to alter my thinking," says the education coordinator. "I was working at my desk on the third floor, and my coworker Tammy sat at the desk across from me. There was a male volunteer downstairs. Other than that, the house was empty. I heard a woman's voice quite clearly say 'Lisa.' It sounded like it might have been someone standing on the stairs just outside the office trying to get my attention." Lisa thought it odd because the stairs are creaky and she had not heard anyone come up the steps. "I figured if there was someone there, they would call again. No one did. So I asked Tammy if she had said my name—she said no." Lisa checked with the volunteer, who confirmed there was no one else in the house.

Tammy then told Lisa that she and another intern heard their names called within the span of a couple of months, shortly after they had joined the staff. "Just once," says Lisa. "It hasn't happened since for any of us. I wish I had known because I would have tried to talk to it. I was so inexperienced; I didn't know to answer. I will if there is a next time."

Could the voice have been the lady in white? Lisa feels it is unlikely because that ghost is usually seen on the main stairs from the first to the second floor. Lisa says some people report feeling a gentle push up the stairs as if someone is helping them along. "It is not a shove, but a guiding hand." No one has seen the spirit long enough or clearly enough to identify it, but they see a feminine shape in a long, white dress. There are records of a woman passing away in the solarium from tuberculosis, and her husband then went on to marry her nurse. Perhaps her spirit is still troubled by her spouse's speedy remarriage.

A recent experience with a visiting medium and her son convinced Lisa that the house also contains the spirit of a child. The woman brought her son along because it was his 10th birthday and she thought it would be an interesting experience for him. "We don't normally do things like that, but there was no one else booked in, and I figured, why not?" says Lisa. The boy and his mother went to the third floor, where the boy kept talking to some unseen child. The medium also got a strong feeling of a child there. Her son said he felt it was a little boy. "He sat down on the floor," Lisa explains, "and rolled a ball toward this spirit child. I saw the ball stop dead still. Then after a pause it rolled back toward her son." Other people have reported feeling the sense of a ball bouncing on the floor. "We know that the McDowells lost a baby and another child. They had 13, and 11 lived."

Down in the basement, where the winter kitchen used to be, there is more unusual activity. "Some people have experienced a feisty slave there," says Lisa. "The first description of this spirit was angry, but a medium suggested it is more forceful, energetic and determined. *Feisty* seems the best description."

In 2006, Lisa began running ghost tours and invited different paranormal investigators to come and gather whatever evidence they could. "It was part of a thematic thing we were doing with all the museums. The theme was 'Oh Lord, Remember Me,' so we had the whole house done in Victorian mourning, complete with caskets, covered mirrors, displays of what to wear if your husband had died…it was just as if there was a death in the house," explains Lisa. "For the first tour we had 50 or 60 people in the house, and I have never seen so many people so happy to stand around and look in the dark."

Teams of paranormal investigators gathered evidence using an extraordinary collection of tools. The team from L.E.M.U.R. Paranormal Investigations, headed by local ghost guru Joshua Warren, brought out a virtual arsenal of equipment from subsonic audio enhancers and night vision goggles to electrostatic generators and temperature gauges in search of proof of active paranormal energy. One of the odd things experienced while investigating was a sudden drain of power from batteries, causing cameras to die. They also found several baffling electromagnetic/electrostatic fields that moved throughout the home. The team concluded that the Smith-McDowell House contains four ghosts and called the museum "one of the most haunted places in Asheville."

Sarah Harrison, founder of the Asheville Paranormal Society, experienced the spooky side of the house during a visit in October 2006. At the time she was working as a camerawoman, assisting a friend who was making a video for the public cable channel. "I went up to the porch to admire the wreath hanging on the door. I tried the door and it was locked, so I went around the side of the house to chat with the L.E.M.U.R. team while we waited for the museum staff to arrive and unlock the door."

Meanwhile, the Channel 24 Fox television crew arrived, went straight to the front door and found it open. "They went inside and heard music playing but couldn't find anyone, so they came out and talked to us," says Sarah. "I thought that was odd, so I went and tried the door again, and it was locked." When the museum employees arrived, they were shocked to hear that the door had been unlocked and that the Fox crew did not set off the motion detectors.

After that, people in the group got good pictures of orbs. Most people felt very uncomfortable in the basement, and there was a member of Sarah's group who thought he saw a ghost of a slave in the back of a storage shed. "Very haunted," she sums up.

Of course, there are always people who feel that ghosts are pure invention meant to draw in unwitting tourists and lovers of the paranormal. Still, the balance weighs in favor of the phantoms. With ghost-hunting now such a high-tech operation, it seems likely that the body of evidence will continue to grow as the ghost hunting tours continue. The museum is open year-round, so it is always a good time to stop by and say hello to Asheville's most spectacular home of the spectral.

Carpe Diem Farms

Highlands, North Carolina

Listen closely to the whispering of the trees on Carpe Diem Farms' 44 acres nestled in the hills of southwestern North Carolina. This farm is not ordinary, and those sounds are not just the rustling leaves.

Owner Sue Blair says her life enrichment center is not so much haunted as a spiritual hub for both the Native

Americans who used to own the land and the animals that lived there. "Over the course of my 12 years on the property, people who have just shown up would say to me, 'Two Feathers is standing here and he wants you to know he's grateful you have raised the consciousness of the property,'" says Sue. She has also received messages from the land's spiritual elders—there is a "grandmother tree" on the property that spoke its wisdom to a visiting psychic.

The woman who visited the property—"a clairvoyant extraordinaire," according to Sue—told her that long ago the land was an educational gathering place for the Cherokee. "She asked me if I noticed the animals standing or moving in circles," Sue says. "I said yes, they do that by the gravesite, and she said it was the Cherokee teaching them. The spirits are working hard to communicate the lessons to the animals that I need to teach to the people who come here."

The animals to which Sue refers are the horses that live on the farm. They are part of the program offered at the center, which has a mission to help individuals "convert life challenges to opportunities." Sue says the animals assist in the teaching—they even offer a course called "In the Company of Horses" in which the horses choose the person they want to work with and then deliver messages to help awaken that person to major issues in their life. "The horses are my guides and spirits that help me to help the people who come to take my classes."

Carpe Diem (which means "seize the day" in Latin) offers workshops, seminars and specialized training for people of all ages. Sue was led by her spirit guides to start the farm at a time when she herself was coping with a messy divorce and trying to find a positive way to move forward.

"I was channeled that I was to do this. I was at a meeting, and suddenly I got this message that I wrote down. Pages and pages of details about starting up an educational foundation and developing an international wellness center And it all flowed. I got non-profit status in record time, found the land, and it just came together. When I first got that message it never occurred to me how big this was to be. It used to overwhelm me, but now I'm in the flow of it. I refuse to live in fear."

But the messages from the native spirits who still walk unseen through the hills and trails of Carpe Diem sometimes need to literally be drummed into the minds of people staying there. Sue recalls how a group of young men residing at the lodge while they helped to build the indoor riding arena in 2008 got a wakeup call they would never forget.

It happened during the Memorial Day holiday weekend, but the lead-up to the story began when the workers moved into the lodge. The five young men did not tune in to the calm, meditative vibe of the place. Instead they drank a lot, played loud music and were generally reckless. "They simply were not being present to the energy here," explains Sue. "They didn't get that this was not just another job."

The young men went home for the long weekend and, upon their return, were shocked to see that the building they had been constructing had completely collapsed. "It went down on the Sunday," says Sue. "All of the trusses were up, but one of the standards that held the first one broke, and like so many dominoes, they all fell. It sounded like an explosion. The owner of the company came to see it and was blown away." The men were told they would have to take it all apart and start over. Sue sat them down and told them that their behavior had been unacceptable to the spirits there and that it was time to honor the land. Then she told them to get to bed because they would need a good night's sleep in order to get started with rebuilding.

The next morning, each of the workers came to see Sue individually to ask who was making all the noise in the middle of the night. It turns out that the men had a sleepless night because they were kept awake by the sound of loud drumming and singing. "The spirits basically set up right on their beds," laughs Sue. "I tried to explain that they were just trying to get the men's attention because they weren't respecting sacred ground. That freaked them out."

The outcome was win-win, according to Sue. The men learned to respect the land and changed their ways. And the farm got a much stronger building. "We're up at 4000 feet in the Blue Ridge Mountains, and we've had hurricanes come through here. This arena can take it."

In addition to the spirits and guides who stay connected to Carpe Diem's land, there are animal spirits that Sue and other guests have seen roaming about. "When I see the animals that have been in my life walk by me, or see them out of the corner of my eye, I know they are still with me," says Sue.

Sue's goal of turning Carpe Diem into an international center for wellness continues to be a work in progress, but she knows from the spirits that surround her that she is on the right track. Because if she wasn't, she is *sure* she would hear about it.

The Foothills Equestrian Nature Center

Tryon, North Carolina

The 380 acres of trails, plus recreational nature and equestrian programs, that make up the Foothills Equestrian Nature Center (FENCE) near Tryon, North Carolina, should be enough to create a lasting impression. It is the only non-profit facility of its kind in the United States—it bridges two states (North and South Carolina)—and its pamphlets proudly boast that practically every day of the year the center hosts "some sort of event for dogs, adults, children, horses and birds."

They left ghosts off the list, perhaps so some of the more skittish visitors are not intimidated, but ghosts are another mainstay of FENCE. All of the center's main buildings, which include an 8000-square-foot house, a barn and an old cabin, appear to be haunted. "The unusual occurrences have been going on pretty much ever since I've been here," says the center's executive director, Melissa Le Roy. And judging by the number of employees and guests who have related tales to her since she joined the organization in 2000, the paranormal shenanigans preceded Melissa by a good many years.

The property has been acquired bit by bit since 1985 when Mrs. Ernst Mahler deeded 112 acres to the newly formed non-profit agency called FENCE. The main buildings used to be the private estate of Jack Kimberly (one of the founders of Kimberly-Clark, the company that manufactures tissues and diapers) and his family. The 8000-square-foot house was built in the early 1930s and now contains offices for the staff, plus two apartments that are original to the house. The apartments used to be the homes of the driver, groundskeeper and nanny.

A third apartment is now in what used to be the barn. "The story of how the barn was remodeled involved the oldest daughter of Jack Kimberly, who married and became pregnant," Melissa explains. "Soon after, her husband was shipped off to World War II, never to return. The daughter, who now had a small child, chose to move back in with her parents. So a new barn was built several hundred yards from the house, and the brick barn adjacent to the home was remodeled into the ground-floor apartment. We have had several accounts of strange happenings from horse show officials who stay in the three apartments. Guests who stay in the ground-floor apartment in the old barn are awakened throughout the night by the sounds of children laughing and running back and forth upstairs in the old hayloft."

The facility also functions as a for-profit venture, running horse shows throughout the year. There are 11 barns with over 300 permanent stalls, four rings, a covered arena and six miles of trails for riders. During competitions, one of the ways that the facility brings in money is to rent out the apartments to judges or riders who wish to stay close to their horse. From April through October the apartments are rented every weekend, so there's plenty of opportunity for the FENCE phantoms to come out and give the guests something extra to remember. "We had one of the maintenance staff half-jokingly tell a family member staying in the apartment to be careful of the ghosts," Melissa recalls. "He got a call from his distraught sister in the morning saying, 'You didn't tell me about these kids who run around laughing and keeping us awake all night.'"

Guests who stay in the two-bedroom apartment next door to the old hayloft are often awakened by the sounds of children running and playing with stick animals that are stored in the grain room. These stick animals have buttons on their ears that you push to play a type of carnival or circus music. One guest, the secretary of a horse show, brought her young son with her for the weekend and awoke to music. She thought that her son might still be up playing his Game Boy, so she went into his room only to find him sound asleep. The music continued to play. She walked around and realized the noise was coming from the room adjacent to hers. Upon entering she noticed that the stick elephant was singing. "The strange thing about this occurrence," says Melissa, "was that owing to other complaints from guests about the music, I had taken the batteries out of all the stick animals. Yet this one was still playing without the batteries."

There have been two sightings of a ghostly figure in the two-bedroom apartment, and both times it was by a female horse show judge staying alone. The first incident, described by a woman from the Dominican Republic, occurred in the middle of the night. She awoke with the intense feeling that someone was staring at her. Half asleep, she could make out the shape of a man standing over her, and as she became more conscious, it appeared he was feeling her forehead as if she was ill. Then the ghost asked her, "Are you feeling better?" The woman reported being so frozen with fear that she couldn't reply or move. The figure then vanished before her eyes. At that point, the woman leaped out of bed, packed her things and left immediately to stay in a hotel.

The second ghost sighting happened about six months later to a judge from Kentucky. "We have no idea who it might be," says Melissa. "We haven't yet researched deaths on the property, though we did find a mysterious graveyard not far from the house with unmarked headstones and foot-stones. It's probably a slave cemetery, but we don't know of any connection to the spirits here."

If you are now thinking that an overnight stay in one of the other apartments might be a better bet for uninter-rupted slumber, think again. Guests in the one-bedroom apartment have reported waking to a bright light that shone down the hallway from the kitchen into the bedroom. When they rise to see what the light is from, they find the refrigerator door standing open. "It's not possible," states Melissa bluntly. "Over the years the building has settled, and the wall that the refrigerator is on has settled a lot, causing you to have to get in between the door and the wall to keep the door open; otherwise it will slam shut." But guests report that they have to push the door hard a couple of times before it will close. Maybe they have to pull the door free from some unseen specter in search of a late night snack.

Staff members also report strange things that happen in the main house. Currently, the center has its nature class-rooms and animal room downstairs. During weekends and holidays, employees take turns feeding the snakes, geckoes and iguana that live in cages. Melissa explains, "We typically keep all the doors locked when entering the building, so we know there is no one else in the building. While downstairs you will hear footsteps upstairs pacing back and forth from the Great Room to the garage as if someone is searching for something. Every time I heard this I would go upstairs and investigate. After about six months of doing that and realizing no one was there, I just got used to the footsteps."

Melinda Leake joined the FENCE team in April 2008 as the executive assistant. It was her turn to feed the animals over the July 4th long weekend. She had no idea at that point that there were ghosts on the premises, but apparently it was time for them to say hello. "When I went downstairs I heard footsteps behind me. Clear as day. Really loud, like big boots coming down the steps," she remembers. "I stopped. The footsteps stopped. I continued, and the footsteps followed me. So now my heart was pounding and the hair on my body was standing up." Then Melinda heard the distinct sound of running back and forth in the hallway. "It was children. You can tell the difference between big and little footsteps, and these were little footsteps. There were several of them running." She went back up to see if she had forgotten to lock the door, but the center was secure. "I thought, okay, that's fine. There's someone else here."

Melinda's experience opened the portal to the paranormal for her at FENCE. Since her first encounter, she says, "To this day I get the coldest feeling, like a bucket of ice water was just dumped on me." The sudden, overwhelming chill causes even the hair on her head to stand up straight. "You can actually feel there is something; you don't know what it is, but there is something there. It's like someone is standing beside me."

Adjacent to the main building is a small log cabin that dates back to the early 1800s. When Jack Kimberly bought the property, there was a larger building on the site that he tore down; he kept only the central part to make a schoolhouse for his children. He put power in it, so it was also used as a place to have parties or weddings. Whatever spirit lingers in the cabin does not like being left in the dark. The glow of lights spilling from the windows has often been seen when the building is supposed to be empty. It happened to Melissa Le Roy one night very late when she stayed to help clean up after a wedding.

"It was after 1 AM," she says, "and as I was driving home I noticed lights were on in the log cabin. I pulled up on the lawn, got out and left my car running, but I must have turned my head for a moment because when I went to walk in I saw that no lights were on. I went inside, flicked them on and off. They worked, so I turned them off, locked the door and walked to my car. When I turned around the lights were on again. I got out of my car and suddenly the lights were off again. I investigated. There wasn't anyone inside—no one playing a joke. So now I thought, this is really weird. When I left the last time the lights stayed off."

Perhaps someone was playing a prank. But when the barn was remodeled, the power to both buildings was disconnected to make safety upgrades. And while the log cabin was powerless, a neighbor who lives on the bordering property would take his dogs for a walk and see lights within. A man named Mr. Dietz noticed lights on in the log cabin; then as he approached, he saw that it looked like candles flickering. As he neared, the light would extinguish itself. When he entered, he reported being able to smell smoke as if someone had just put out a candle. However, no one appeared to be in the cabin, and neither Mr. Dietz nor his dogs picked up on the presence of anyone running away. It seems that even spirits like a little light to keep away the dark.

The strangest thing that ever happened to Melissa Le Roy took place in the fall of 2005. It was a day that she was alone at the center, and it was a typical fall day: cool, overcast and drizzling. Early in the afternoon the front door chime went off, letting her know someone had entered the lobby. She discovered "a really sweet old lady" who stated that she had just moved to Tryon Estates (a large retirement community in Polk County). The elderly woman said that several of the residents told her to visit FENCE because she loved hiking. She had come to pick up a trail map and more information on the center. Melissa recalls, "While we were standing in front of the large aerial map of the facility I proceeded to give her my elevator speech about FENCE. She was constantly looking behind me down the hall." Melissa didn't let it bother her, thinking maybe the woman was one of many people who cannot maintain eye contact. But it was much more than that.

"After I had finished my speech she said to me, 'Do you realize you have two female spirits behind you?' I simply replied, 'Really?' but I was thinking, oh great. She went on to say that they told her they were very happy with what I had done to restore the wood floors. At this point the hair on my arms was standing up." In 2000, when Melissa first came to work at FENCE, the lobby, stairs and hallway were carpeted. In the winter of 2003, she removed the carpet and refinished the wood floors. "I thought to myself, how could she have known this when she just moved here to this area this month?" Trying to act normally, Melissa gave the visitor brochures, a calendar and a trail map. She also encouraged her to sign the mailing list.

Melissa sent out a note the next day to follow up. "The strange thing is that the note came back—no such person at this address. I sat there at my desk staring at the note. Then I contacted several of our board members and volunteers who live at Tryon Estates. No one knew of her. And further, the apartment she listed as her residence had been vacant for several months since the last occupant [a male] had passed away. I have never been able to find the sweet, old lady."

Melissa remains unfazed by the phantoms. She is not only fine with them, but she would also love to know more about them. "It never bothers me. I sleep here all the time."

The Trans-Allegheny Lunatic Asylum

Weston, West Virginia

Creepy. Intimidating. Haunted. That about sums up the Trans-Allegheny Lunatic Asylum (TALA) in Weston, West Virginia. Thousands of patients were admitted within its blue sandstone walls in the 113 years of its operation; hundreds died there. Many of them still languish in the wards and treatment rooms of the dilapidated structure. This place is not for the faint of heart.

"For a feeling of being absolutely overwhelmed and intimidated, it's hard to beat the Trans-Allegheny Lunatic Asylum," says Patricia Marin, who is a part-time ghost hunter. "You can't help but feel tempted to turn back before it's too late."

The asylum is now in private hands, and ghost hunters and paranormal investigation teams are encouraged to explore the dankest, darkest corners of the massive building. There is a long list of eerie phenomena to keep them coming back. They have recorded apparition sightings, disembodied voices, screams and disturbing sounds, people being touched or pulled, footsteps and the sound of children running in hallways.

"I knew that the fourth floor was haunted because I used to have to go up there for medical records," former hospital employee Sue Parker told one reporter. "I could hear them following me." Sue worked for three decades as a psychiatric aide and in the admissions department. "I've seen it before and I've heard it before."

In an interview dated May 1, 2008, Sue remembers seeing a man in the area of the hospital segregated for female patients only. "He was there," she said. "The patients kept saying they saw the man. He was leaning back against the wall with his arms crossed. The doors were locked with no way in or out. But security didn't find a man."

How did this massive mental hospital end up with a reputation as one of the most haunted health facilities in the United States? It was designed to be a sanctuary using the curative effects of architecture to improve the lives of the mentally ill, but in the end it was an over-crowded, run-down pit of despair, and many of the patients who entered were destined to die there.

Looking like a storybook castle, the asylum must have been imposing and somewhat ominous with its gargoyles and 200-foot spire off the central clock tower when it was finished in 1881. It is the largest hand-cut stone masonry building in North America and worldwide is second only in size to Moscow's Kremlin.

Architect Richard Andrews designed the huge, rambling edifice based on the Kirkbride plan. The premise was that long, staggered wings would ensure patients received an abundance of fresh air and sunlight. But in reality, the asylum pre-dated psychotropic drugs or other psychiatric therapies, and behavior modification was really the only treatment known. That meant many patients spent years—or a lifetime—confined in a tiny, cell-like room. They were caged to protect themselves and others.

And let's be clear—the late 1800s was a time when people could be committed for afflictions as nebulous as laziness, egotism, disappointed love, female disease, mental excitement, cold, novel reading, greediness, desertion by husband, gathering in the head, exposure and quackery, jealousy and religion, asthma, and bad habits and policital excitement, just to name a few. The first patient to be admitted was a housekeeper from Ohio who apparently suffered from "domestic trouble."

Treatments progressed to include electric shock and lobotomies (dubious advancements, one might argue), and the hospital became a victim of its own success. Originally designed to house 250 patients, it held a staggering 2400 people by the 1950s. The conditions deteriorated to somewhere between horrific and appalling. By the mid-1990s, the dilapidated state of the building, plus changes in how mental health was treated, resulted in the forced closure of what was by then called the Weston State Hospital.

The building sat empty until 2007. For 14 years, the tormented spirits of former patients freely roamed the two and a half miles of corridors and peered out the 921 windows until their domain was bought by Rebecca Jordan-Gleason and her family for $1.5 million in an auction on the steps of the Lewis County courthouse.

"I never thought we would be getting ghosts with the deal," the energetic owner says. "We were looking at it primarily for historic tours. We initially thought about making it a hotel but have decided to keep it as it is." Rebecca credits her father for saving the massive complex. "The rumor was out that it was going to be torn down, and my dad didn't want to see it come down." Her father had been instrumental in saving another historic property and felt compelled to step in and protect West Virginia's history again.

As for the ghosts, Rebecca knew of the stories but never thought much of them. "People had been telling stories forever." Then she was contacted by The Atlantic Paranormal Society (TAPS). "We invited them in to check it out, and they sent me some really cool stuff but I still wasn't convinced. We had some more ghost hunters come in—we made no claims!—but we had two all-female groups come for a night." And it was on that occasion that Rebecca converted from skeptic to believer. "I was doing security on the fourth floor, and suddenly I had every single door on the ward shut on me at the same time. It was like thunder. Everyone came running. If I hadn't just used the bathroom I would have had an accident," she laughs.

So Rebecca embraced the notion of having a haunted hospital and, while getting busy with renovations, also opened the facility up to the public for ghost tours and paranormal investigators. She has since become familiar with the specters that populate the asylum. "We have Jacob, Lily, the shadow guy on the fourth floor, the angry nurse—we've had multiple people able to contact them. We had about 50 ghost hunts last year. We've had mediums come in, and that's really cool. Without reviewing any of the stuff we have, they come through and name patients that I match up with cemetery records."

On May 2, 2008, TAPS declared the mental hospital to be officially haunted. Jason Hawes and Grant Wilson visited with all their gear, including high-tech recording equipment, and recorded sounds that they claim are clear indicators of paranormal activity. In one recording they captured what sounds like female laughter, and they also recorded a voice that told them to "go home."

Grant told one interviewer that the investigators intended to debunk the reports of unusual activity, like stories of hearing gurneys move down hallways and screams from inside the former shock therapy room. Instead they discovered signs of "an intelligent haunting"—a spirit that is actively trying to communicate with the living. In a video posted by TAPS on YouTube, the men can be heard (not really seen as they are in total darkness) interviewing a sad spirit named Jake and making contact with the nasty nurse. In the interview Jake communicates by way of generating a flash in a K-2 meter and indicates that there are 11 spirits in the place.

Two other members of TAPS saw a shadow that appeared to be crouching with its hands over its head as if to ward off a blow before "being sucked out of the room."

For the past year and a half Anthony Prunty has led the nighttime ghost hunts, but he admits that he only became a believer quite recently. Prior to that, despite the eerie surroundings, Anthony found solace in logic. "I was always a sceptic about the ghosts because this place is full of shadows." He cited an example of a deer getting in one night when a door was left open. "You see something out of the corner of your eye, but really, what was it?" But in February 2009 he witnessed something that "proves logic wrong."

During a shift as tour guide for a ghost hunting expedition, Anthony was walking down one of the wards on the second floor to check on his group when he saw a silhouette of light coming from a back window of the ward. He thought it must be from a flashlight from someone in the group. Then it got strange. "I saw something *in* the light poke outside a door and look at me. It was the shape of a man in a crouched down position. I saw it run across the hallway diagonally into a supply closet with no exits." Anthony checked with his group, thinking one of them had run across the hall, but there was no one missing. So he grabbed one of their flashlights and hurried down to check the closet. It was empty. "There was no way anything could have gotten out without me seeing," insists Anthony. "That incident made a believer out of me. It was inexplicable."

About a month prior to Anthony's conversion, he witnessed a similar change in a fellow tour guide. The two had just dropped off their groups and were alone in the ward, walking along and talking when all of a sudden the other fellow bolted. "Suddenly I see him charging in a full-fledged run out of the ward," recalls Anthony. When he finally found his frightened colleague, the other guide said that as they were walking he heard someone say threateningly in his ear, "Get out of my building!" He even felt breath on his ear, and that is what sent him running.

Most recently, on a Saturday night ghost tour, Anthony stepped out on the second-floor balcony to have a cigarette, leaving both doors to the balcony open. One of the other team leaders joined him to ask a question, so he turned to answer her. "I was facing the doors, and as I talked to her I watched one door start to close very slowly, then in a split second it just slammed shut," says Anthony. They shone lights into the room and could not see anything, then the second door slammed shut. Okay, that's scary. But there's more.

Anthony tells me, "From somewhere nearby we heard a blood-curdling scream—I think it was a woman's voice it was so high—and a door slammed shut." The ghost hunters had an electronic voice phenomena (EVP) recorder set up in the room, and when they listened back to the digital recording, the team was stunned by what they had captured. "You could hear the first door slam, footsteps on the hardwood, then the next door slam, then you hear me say, 'What was that?' Then you hear the scream, and it was even more blood curdling, like someone was being stabbed or raped. Then you hear a ghost hunter say, 'Let's go check that out.' And right away there is a voice that says very clearly, 'No, don't go down there.' That voice sounded like it was right beside us, but none of us heard it at the time."

Astonished by their experience, the group went in search of the other people in the building to see if they heard either the doors slam or the scream. "In this place, you can usually hear a pin drop from the other end of the ward," says Anthony. "And yet they didn't hear anything."

With eerie experiences happening nearly every week, Rebecca now keeps a log of the events with the intention of writing her own book about TALA's spirited world. She sent me the list, and it reads like a sci-fi thriller: cold spots, shadows that move through people or along halls, and guides being touched, tickled, grabbed, pulled or pushed. Then there are the screams, groans, whispers, laughter, talking, footsteps, doors locking or unlocking, lights flickering and the sound of gurneys moving across the floor. For people who bring equipment, there are spikes in the meter readings, inexplicable malfunctions or battery failure, photographs of orbs and lots of EVPs.

With the help of mediums, psychics and paranormal investigators, there is a growing list of ghosts that have been identified. Lily is the ghost of a young girl about age nine who wears a white dress and is seen on the second floor. She reportedly kissed a two-year-old toddler on the cheek. A former patient known as Old Ruth still haunts Ward C, where she was held with the more violent female inmates. She also makes her presence known on Ward 1, where she was transferred after injuring herself. Sue Parker was pushed against the wall by an unseen force after walking through the ward calling Ruth's name.

Apparitions of nurses in white uniforms and in Civil War–era uniforms have been seen. One little girl saw a man "in a pin stripe suit, with short hair, big buttons on the suit, brown tie boots up to his knees, and a long beard" staring at her. According to the evidence book kept by TALA staff, hundreds of people have seen a sourceless shadow in one of the hallways: "the shadow moved against the wall and darted into three doorways and up to a couple. The couple felt a presence in between them."

Rebecca hasn't given up on the idea of adding a hotel to the business. "In 10 years or so we would like to convert a building on the property to a hotel. We also have 300 acres of grounds, so we may add an amusement feature. Might I say, it was a steal at $1.5 million!"

There is a two-hour evening tour for the adventurous, and guides make sure to hit the four "hot spots" of the asylum.

They advise visitors to bring along cameras, digital recorders, electromagnetic field meters and any other gadget or gizmo that will record the presence of spirit energy. They also encourage groups to stick together—because you never know what lurks inside the old seclusion cells in the farthest reaches of the hospital.

The Moundsville Penitentiary

Moundsville, West Virginia

The great thing about the fortress known as one of the bloodiest prisons in the United States is that it not only looks haunted, it *is* haunted—big time. Apparitions. Orbs. Shadow men. Screams. Footsteps. For lovers of the paranormal, this former jail should be on the list of "must see" places.

Moundsville Penitentiary is the gothic epitome of grim. It is *Shawshank Redemption* meets *Friday the Thirteenth*. The real-life horror show that played out at 818 Jefferson Avenue continues to provide fodder for ghost enthusiasts because so many tortured souls died in unspeakable ways during the 119 years that the jail operated. From 1889 to 1950, prisoners were hanged. The electric chair took over until the death penalty was abolished in 1965. But executions account for only 85 of the 998 men who died there. Murders, suicides, riots and cruel punishments on instruments of torture such as the "Kicking Jenny" and the "Shoo-Fly" contributed to the violent deaths of hundreds of men. Many of those souls now roam freely through the hallways and cell blocks.

"Inmates are a suspicious bunch," explains Paul Kirby of the Moundsville Economic Development Council. The MEDC now operates the national historic site, offering tours including overnight ghost hunts. "Inmates didn't want to die here because they feared their soul would never leave. It is still a belief with prisoners in newer institutions. And maybe there's something to it."

The castle-style stone structure, with its 24-foot-high walls, turrets and battlements, opened in 1876 in Moundsville because it was close to what was then the state capitol in Wheeling. It was only meant to house 480 prisoners, but by the 1930s there were 2400 inmates squeezed into every last space. Crowding only added to the inhumanity and brutality. At times, three men were confined to a five- by seven-foot cell.

Back in the 1930s, the first of the ghost sightings was already taking place—guards spotted an inmate walking by the wall outside of the maintenance area. They sounded the general alarm and investigated, but no one was there. Former guard Ed Littell told a television crew that, during his more than 20 years working all three shifts up in the guard tower, he saw shadows and heard noises. He would send a yard officer to check it out, but there was never anyone around.

In 1995, the doors closed permanently. The West Virginia Supreme Court ruled that the small cells, violence and deplorable conditions amounted to "cruel and unusual punishment." The prisoners are gone, but the people now running the institution say they are far from forgotten. "They won't harm you, but they might startle you," says Tom Stiles, internal coordinator of operations for West Virginia Penitentiary Tours.

There are several hot spots of paranormal activity: the shower cages, the chapel, Death Row, the North Wagon Gate, the Sugar Shack, and the basement of the administration building. The Sugar Shack had anything but a sweet reputation. During bad weather when the inmates could not go outside for their recreational break, they used this area in the basement. The guards left prisoners largely unsupervised, and though no deaths are recorded in the Shack, many prisoners were beaten, raped or otherwise abused. The North Wagon Gate is where prisoners awaited death by hanging. And in one dark corner of the basement, a known snitch met his end at the hands of vengeful prisoners who fashioned homemade knives and stabbed him to death.

Polly Gear works as a volunteer paranormal guide, and for the past 10 years she has walked people through the extremely creepy parts of the prison at night. She can cite several inexplicable experiences, such as seeing a headless apparition in prison uniform go through a wall. She has heard men crying and wailing in the psychiatric ward, and in the dental room in the medical area she recorded a man's voice saying "splendid" to one of the group members on her tour. "I have seen a lot of different shadows in the psychiatric ward and infirmary, heard lots of footsteps, lots of screaming and yelling," she says. "It is so amazing to experience this when you know you are the only people in the cell block and you hear men talking or crying.

"In the North Hall area I had my hair pulled and was touched on the arms and legs. Last year we went into the new cells, closed the doors behind us, walked in 10 feet and the door opened and closed again," Polly tells me. "Then we heard a man say, 'I'm Jimmy.' I tried to talk to him, but he mumbled and then it faded away."

On one occasion Polly and her group saw an arm reaching through the cell bars. They have seen flashes of light, balls of light and white mist. In the Sugar Shack, Polly threw a pack of cigarettes on the floor and told the spirits, "Here you go." A voice heard on a digital recording said, "You have tobacco on you." Polly was not surprised. "They do know what we say." She has tried to tell the imprisoned spirits that they can leave, but she gets answers like, "We belong here."

The most amazing incident for Polly occurred five years into her stint at the prison when she took a picture of the shadow man. In May 2004, she was by herself walking through a hallway on her way to the lobby when she heard a noise behind her. Returning to where she heard the sound, she turned on her flashlight for a better look. "And there it was walking right toward me, looking out the windows, unaware that I was there," recalls Polly. "It was the exact shape of a man about 6' 4", but inside the form it was moving black static. I had a three-quarter view, but there were no facial features or hair."

As the shadow walked toward Polly, it walked "like a jerky animated cartoon" but seemed aware of its surroundings. "When I put my flashlight on it, that's when it noticed light on its arm. Then it looked around, looked at me, got scared and jumped over by the doorway."

Polly threw her flashlight down and walked backward about 110 feet all the way down the hall. Meanwhile, she was digging out her camera. "I held it out in the dark, took one shot and it was there." Although the shadow man appeared to be running out the door, Polly thinks it may have looked back when she turned on her camera. "It makes a musical sound when it starts up, and he may have wondered what that was."

Polly put her picture on the internet after showing staff at the penitentiary. "There is no way to know what it was," she explains, "but I put it on the web because I saw it with my own eyes."

Tour guide Lori O'Neil also knows there is something paranormal inside the prison. "We all start out as sceptics, wanting to believe but not really sure until something happens. On the night tours, I've seen grown men cry and run from the building. One man said he was shoved hard from behind in the infirmary, but there was nothing there. He ran out and was desperate to be let outside."

Lori gets a lot of emails from people wanting to share their experiences once they are safely home and away from the property. She also contributes to the growing body of evidence that Moundsville is actively haunted. "When I am the only person in the building at night I hear footsteps, and cell doors slam shut—and they are electric, so there is no way to close them manually, but somehow they do close."

Lori admits that the place can make the mind work over-time and play tricks on perception. But then there is what happened during the Halloween haunted house tour in 2008. The prison sets up for a special ghost tour, complete with fog and strobe lights. Lori worked at the entrance and watched as one tour group started through the haunted house toward the Sugar Shack. "One person from the tour left the group and walked back toward me. I said, 'You need to rejoin the group.' But he just disappeared before my eyes."

Paranormal investigators and mediums have all gathered information that seems to corroborate the stories and confirm the known hot spots. The investigators' recording devices pick up a lot of electronic voice phenomena in the infirmary and down in the basement where the snitch was murdered. Some psychics or people sensitive to energy refuse to go down there. Polly Gear agrees that the area is "oppressive and filled with negative feelings."

Another doubter turned believer is Tom Stiles, the internal coordinator of operations. He started in 2000, thinking the ghost tours were interesting and unique. "I was pretty sceptical of it all. I even came and spent a few nights, and nothing happened. I went along with it, though, because it was good for business."

Then in 2007 Tom discovered what all the hype was about. During a week-long shoot with a film crew doing a paranormal show, Tom stayed each night to make sure things went smoothly. On the Wednesday night, a thunder and lightning storm raged the entire evening. Finally, at 2:30 AM they decided to wrap for the night because it was too noisy. Tom had loaned the crew his computer monitor to watch what the cameras were recording, so when they decided to quit he sent a technician to unhook the monitor and return it to his office. Tom heard the man exclaim when he saw what was on the screen. "There was a four-foot-long light bar, about four inches in diameter, moving back and forth across the lawn," says Tom.

"We watched it for five or six minutes, and others in the crew came to watch too. Finally six of us said, 'We need to see what this is,' so we went out in the pouring rain to where the camera was. And we could see this vertical light bar moving as if it was pacing around the lawn." The light moved back and forth for some time, then moved over to the stairwell leading into the building. "We could see it descend one step at a time," recalls Tom. "Then it dissipated into a gray mass, not human form but a dense, floating, gray mass; it hovered there for three or four seconds and then moved inside the building. We all could see it as plain as anything."

The gray mass moved into an area of the prison near the Sugar Shack. "I was just awestruck," admits Tom. "Now I'm thinking maybe there is something to this. It changed my feelings on the whole paranormal thing."

About six weeks after that came the moment that convinced Tom beyond any doubt that spirits stay entangled in the prison. He was constructing the haunted house along with Lori O'Neil and her husband, who were busy in another part of the prison. Tom was working alone in the Sugar Shack. "I was walking through carrying a handful of tools, and I felt something hit me on the arm as if it wanted me to stop. It startled me."

Tom put the tools down on floor and went to turn the light on, but there was nothing there for him to walk into. The area was wide open. "That threw me. It affected me emotionally a little bit. I kind of hurried to the other area where Lori and her husband were and said it was time to go."

Lori remembers the day. "He came running, and you knew something had happened just by the look on his face. It rattled me, too, that he had been touched. Not much startles him, so to see him that upset…I was ready to go too."

And so, it seems that some of the prisoners who served time for heinous crimes may still be working off their debt to society, as afterlife attractions. West Virginia Penitentiary Tours invites anyone with a penchant for the paranormal to sign up for the ghost tours—though be warned, they fill up fast. Paul Kirby says they sell out almost as soon as they go on sale. Ghosts are apparently big business.

Tennessee's Haunted Cemeteries

Jobe Cemetery, Erwin

In the Tennessee town of Erwin, right along Main Street is a cemetery that many people say is haunted by a nasty spirit nicknamed "Old Dawg." And although some ghost hunters say looking for otherworldly entities in a cemetery is a little like shooting fish in a barrel, the Jobe Cemetery does seem like a good bet for spotting apparitions because the spirits of several murdered men are said to walk among the more than 500 tombstones.

The reason for the large number of male spirits is connected to the town's history with homeless people. Railroad hoboes gathered in Erwin because they could easily hitch rides on the Clinchfield railroad. The community of men would congregate in a wooded area near the cemetery, away from the prying eyes of local residents. During the day, many of them shuffled into town to panhandle or work odd jobs for food, and at night they reconvened at the clearing. Some of the men liked to play cards and drink, and the explosive combination of poverty, gambling and alcohol often resulted in violence that sometimes turned deadly.

Of all the legends, the most enduring is that of Old Dawg, a huge, angry man so-called because his heavily lined face resembled that of a bloodhound. His demeanor was more like that of a hungry wolf, though, snarling and bloodthirsty. Old Dawg did not like to lose at cards and would kill anyone who bested him at a game. No information is available as to how he died, but Old Dawg's apparition has been spotted numerous times trudging through the graves of the Jobe Cemetery.

In his book *Haunted Tennessee,* Charles Edwin Price tells how a group of young school-age boys in the 1920s went out to the cemetery one night, despite adult warnings to avoid the place, and waited in the bushes to see the infamous ghost. Of course, none of the boys wanted to leave for fear of looking "yellow-bellied," but most of them ran the minute they spotted the shape of a colossal man moving toward them. One boy, paralyzed with fear, stayed rooted to the spot while the horrible hulk of a man with no pupils in his eyes and razor-sharp, rotting teeth growled that he was going to kill the boy. As the youngster covered his head and cowered with fear, he felt a sharp, cold chill pass through his body. When he raised his eyes, the apparition was gone. And he lived to tell the tale.

So the best advice might be to take a trip to this quaint, historic site, but beware of the Jobe Cemetery after dark. After all, there is no point messing with an Old Dawg.

Jonesborough Cemetery, Jonesborough

What could incite a ghost to ignore its well-marked resting place and haunt a grave miles away? Because that seems to be the situation at the Jonesborough Cemetery in eastern Tennessee. The ghost of William Gannaway Brownlow is quite well known as the phantom that frequently wanders through the city's graveyard.

This is the same William G. Brownlow—noted editor of the *Jonesborough Whig,* Methodist minister, Union supporter during the Civil War and U.S. senator—who has a gravestone bearing his name in Knoxville's Old Gray Cemetery (see below). So it is a strange thing that Parson Brownlow (reviled by many people in the area for his aggressively opinionated nature) haunts a different burial plot than his own.

Dr. Nancy Acuff, a retired East Tennessee State University professor, studies the supernatural and knows well the eerie goings-on in the oldest city in the state. In an interview for the *Johnson City Press,* Dr. Acuff says of Brownlow, "He was a real fire-and-brimstone type of minister. The thing that is puzzling is why his ghostly image has been seen here."

Dr. Acuff has a theory as to why the minister and zealous abolitionist paces through the pathways of Jonesborough's cemetery at night; she believes that the answer may lie in Brownlow's personal life. She heard that one of the notorious newspaperman's wives is buried in the Jonesborough Cemetery, and Dr. Acuff thinks he comes to visit his wife's gravesite.

Another theory is connected to his work as minister during the horrific typhoid and cholera outbreaks in the 1800s. Brownlow is reported to have conducted mass burials of five and six victims of the disease at a time. Perhaps the crude and rushed nature of the work offended his spirit, and he has returned to grant the individuals a more personal—if somewhat belated—farewell. Maybe "better late than never" is true even in the spirit world.

Old Gray Cemetery, Knoxville

The Curfeu tolls the Knell of parting Day,
The lowing Herd winds slowly o'er the Lea,
The Plowman homeward plods his weary Way,
And leaves the World to Darkness, and to me.
Now fades the glimmering Landscape on the Sight,
And all the Air a solemn Stillness holds;

Save where the Beetle wheels his droning Flight,
And drowsy Tinklings lull the distant Folds.

—Thomas Gray (1716–1771),
"Elegy Written in a Country Churchyard"

The Old Gray Cemetery in Knoxville, Tennessee, is no ordinary graveyard. Its elegant memorial spires mingle with unmarked graves, and centuries-old trees with long, weeping branches sweep the tombstones in a way that seems to protect but also haunt the grounds. Even during daylight hours, this place feels spooky.

The land bordered by Broadway, Tyson and Cooper streets was purchased in 1850, though it was not dedicated until two years later when the first 40 lots were sold in a public auction. Citizens of the time struggled to find a suitable name for their new cemetery. Finally, Henrietta Reese, the wife of Judge William B. Reese, the first president of the cemetery's board of trustees, suggested naming the graveyard in honor of English poet Thomas Gray because his poem "Elegy Written in a Country Churchyard" so aptly described the beauty and essence of the burial ground.

Today, 13 acres of solemn gray stones date back 150 years, many with names that suggest a broad pedigree of the past. Among the names of note carved into the heavy granite are William G. Brownlow—Tennesse governor, senator and renowned newspaper editor—along with several other U.S. senators and congressmen, more than two dozen Knoxville mayors, judges, artists, writers, suffragettes, industrialists, educators, military leaders, physicians and philosophers. At least one spirit is restless, roaming the winding pathways at night. Seen by many, and in some cases heard, the mysterious black shape has no name other than "black aggie."

Very little is known of the black shape despite numerous investigations by local ghost hunters. Is it really a lost soul, or is it a hoax? A team from Knox Paranormal Investigators says it is real. The group recorded an electronic voice phenomenon (EVP) in answer to the question, "Why do you walk around here?" They posted their recording on YouTube, convinced they connected to the free-ranging spirit. Although it is hard to make out, they interpret the response they got to be, "Free."

Meanwhile, other spirits keep things interesting while groups wait around to spot the shadow figure. Andrea Jamison of Spirit Hunters of Knoxville (SHOK) proudly posted two images of what she says are full body apparitions taken with digital cameras at the cemetery. "One is the old caretaker who died in the 1960s," says Andrea. "We had it confirmed by someone who grew up in the area and identified the image as that of Big Joe. He is even carrying his lantern." Also pointing to the caretaker as a resident spirit is an EVP that the SHOK team recorded in which Andrea's husband John can be heard shaking a hand warmer, and a voice mumbles something. The other investigators can then be heard asking John what he said—but John didn't say anything. "When we ran the tape through our program, you can hear that the voice says, 'Where's my hammer?'"

The other apparition photographed by SHOK is that of a woman with long hair. "We got it two different times in two different places," says Andrea. "We worked with a sensitive who was able to tell me why she was there. The woman was a schoolteacher, and she is watching over the kids buried in the cemetery."

SHOK's crew intends to try again to contact the black mass that so many people claim to have seen. "Some say it is a non-human entity," Andrea states, "but we think it is a shadow person. We would really like to find out. But it is a 13-acre cemetery, and that's a lot of ground to cover."

In December 2003, the East Tennessee Paranormal Society roamed the old cemetery and, instead of a black aggie, investigator Eric Huckabee roped in an old wrangler. He captured an image on his digital camera of what they believe is the spirit of Herb Evers, a Knoxville cowboy who died in a shoot-out in Market Square. Evers is said to have initiated the city's first and only duel with a neighbor who was messing with Evers' sheep. But the cowboy lost and, as a result, his rankled spirit continues to roam Old Gray trying to even the score by finding someone to spook.

What haunts the somber, sullen stones of this cemetery? Is there a shapeless shadow lost in this world? Or have too many imaginations been affected by the wind through the trees and the Victorian architecture? Why not spend a night amid the tombstones and find out?

5
More Haunted Hotels

The Grove Park Inn Resort & Spa

Asheville, North Carolina

When part of training new employees includes a briefing on the resident ghost, you know that the Grove Park Inn Resort & Spa in Asheville, North Carolina, takes its mysterious Pink Lady seriously. And why not? For more than half a century, hotel staff and guests have been tickled, hugged and teased by the playful phantom. There are so many accounts of encounters with the frothy pink mist that it is hard to know where to start. Perhaps the best place is at the beginning.

The stories originate with the death of a young woman in the 1920s. She was a guest at the hotel back in the days when the hotel roster included names such as Harry Houdini, George Gershwin, Thomas Edison, Henry Ford and Eleanor Roosevelt. She stayed in the same room as F. Scott Fitzgerald—though not at the same time. Unfortunately, the unnamed guest of room 545 did not check out in the regular fashion. The woman dressed in pink either fell or was pushed to her death, landing on the Palm Court atrium floor. This last information was gathered by the hotel in 1996 during an intensive study by a local team of paranormal investigators.

Derrek Swing trains the new employees at the Grove Park Inn and spends a few minutes of his two-day orientation giving trainees the low-down on the Pink Lady. "It's kind of unavoidable here in Asheville," says Derrek. "Most people have grown up knowing about our ghosts, so it's one of those things where it's better to talk about it rather than hide it. I have fun with it." In his 11-plus years at the hotel, Derrek has not seen the Pink Lady and is "not completely convinced" she exists but adds that many of the stories he hears are completely believable. "I'm open to the idea of it being a possibility," he says.

Included in the orientation tour for new employees are a few choice stories that have been relayed to Derrek by people he feels are reliable sources. One of the stories that stands out for him occurred in either the late 1990s or the early 2000s. A young female guest staying in room 545 woke in the middle of the night to a cold breeze and a noise in the room. She got up to discover that the outside windows were open. Thinking she must have failed to latch them properly, she shut them and went back to bed. A short time later, she woke again to the same thing—only this time, she knew it wasn't her fault. Feeling unnerved, she got up and shut them again and eventually fell back to sleep. The next day while checking out, she told the front desk person that her stay had been good except for the windows opening up on her. "This is the best part," Derrek says enthusiastically. "She went on to say that she had also had a wild dream that she fell off the balcony in her room. The guest was not aware of the Pink Lady prior to staying here."

Tales such as seeing a flowing cloud of pink smoke or experiencing bone-chilling cold in room 545 have circulated for as long as anyone can remember. Derrek has looked into the history and says that though he has not been able to find any hard facts about who the Pink Lady may have been, there are articles about sightings that date back to the early 1940s. One clear pattern to the stories is that the spirit is gentle, kid-friendly and a little mischievous at times.

Jay Winer, the inn's director of public relations, told me of an incident when a family with a young boy stayed in room 545 without knowing anything of the room's reputation. The hotel was undergoing extensive renovations at the time. The next morning, the lad told an astounded concierge about how he woke up in the middle of the night and "there was a really nice lady" telling him about all the rooms being built. The lady said she wanted to show him, but, the young boy continued, she walked through the wall and he couldn't follow her.

One of the hotel's managers told Derrek Swing of a similar incident in which she was earning some extra money babysitting for guests in the hotel. The family was out for the night and she had put their son to bed, but she could hear him talking as if having a conversation with someone. When the parents returned, the little boy woke up and very excitedly told his parents and the babysitter that he had been playing with "a nice lady."

Guests are more likely to feel the Pink Lady than to speak with her. One woman fell asleep on top of the bed covers in room 545 only to awake to the sensation of someone tickling her toes. The hotel's current engineering facilities manager shared an experience with a painter who worked in room 545 during the late 1950s—they both felt an icy chill so intense that they refused to enter the room again.

Kathy Urbin of Blountville, Tennessee, spent a night at the Grove Park Inn in 1998 with her husband and two daughters.

She awoke around midnight to noises from the adjoining room, the sounds of people banging about, and she assumed it was a late check-in. To get herself back to sleep, she reached for her husband's hand and clung to its warmth for security. But it dawned on her that her husband was to her right, and the hand she was holding was on her left. Kathy looked over expecting to see one of her daughters, but there was no one there. As she took that in, simultaneously the sensation of warmth ceased. She mentioned the noise to a front desk clerk the next day and was equally astonished to hear that no one occupied the adjoining room. After reading up on the hotel's unique history, Kathy concluded that she must have been holding the Pink Lady's hand.

Another guest wrote in an online blog on January 13, 2008, that she had a somewhat similar experience to Kathy Urbin. The woman stayed at the hotel in room 544 for a week-long meeting in March 1997. She shared her room with a colleague, and for two nights they slept undisturbed. But on the third night, just after midnight, they heard alarming sounds coming from the room next door. She writes, "We thought our 'neighbors' were hurling the furniture against the wall, smashing glass and throwing each other around. We heard a door slamming repeatedly and loud thuds, as if a human was hitting the floor and walls." Naturally, the two women thought it best to call the front desk and report the cacophony for fear someone might be hurt. But as they prepared to dial, the noise stopped. The next morning, the desk clerk tried to explain the sounds away as part of the hotel's renovation without mentioning the possibility of a ghost. "At midnight?" the woman asked. That day, the woman found a book in the gift shop explaining the history.

There were no more late-night sounds, but the woman had one more eerie encounter. It was time to check out, and she was loading up a baggage cart in her room. She grabbed her last bag from the washroom, and suddenly "the room went cold—absolutely freezing! The temperature drop was so dramatic that I literally froze in my tracks." The Pink Lady must have a sense of humor because as the woman stood paralyzed, the television turned on and started running through the channels. "You have never seen a woman with a loaded baggage cart move as fast as I did to get out of that room."

The Pink Lady does occasionally travel outside room 545. A lawyer named Bob Farrar, devout nonbeliever of the paranormal, told a reporter at the *Mountain Xpress* that his encounter with the Pink Lady in 2001 made a believer of him. The Georgia native describes receiving a hug while having a massage at the inn's spa, which had just opened. Bob says that as he lay on the table with his eyes closed, he felt a gentle hug first on his right shoulder. "Then I felt them put their arms around my neck and [gently] squeeze." The sensation startled him into opening his eyes, only to discover that the massage therapist was working down at his feet. "So it couldn't have been her," concluded Bob. For the former skeptic, it was a life altering moment. "I would swear under oath what I experienced," reported the attorney, who also declares that he does not drink or use drugs.

In the fall of that same year, the Pink Lady made her presence felt in the hotel atrium. Guest Mike Mooney walked through the atrium on the night he arrived to buy a drink from one of the vending machines. It was around 11 PM, and he was alone. He noticed that the room "felt heavy" as he entered it but paid little attention. However, as he walked out with his soda, he felt the hair on the left side of his body suddenly bristle as he passed an old bench chair. At the same time he felt a tug on his left ear. Was the Pink Lady inviting him to join her for a drink? Mike did not want to find out. "I ran like hell back to the room."

On March 17, 1999, one of the managers logged this entertaining entry: "9:10 PM. Spent a good bit of time speaking to Mr. Phillips Rm 421 about his encounter tonight with the Pink Lady. Guest stated he was taking a bath at 7:30 PM tonight and witnessed a female figure dressed in 'rosy-pink' move quickly past the bathroom door, pausing to look in at him. He stated he was startled and angry and intended to call the FD [front desk] to complain about someone in his room but went on to dinner…instead." Mr. Phillips repeated his story later at the front desk and, far from being upset, he was excited enough to plan a return trip with his fiancée for later that summer.

In the hotel's hand-out given to guests who express an interest in the ghost, there are several other fascinating stories, such as the police chief who swears he felt someone sit beside him on the bed in his room while he made a telephone call, or the employees who saw the Pink Lady visit the accounting office after a New Year's Eve party. They told management, "We heard someone come in the back door. We looked up and she went by real fast—a woman dressed in party clothes. We thought it was a guest, so we got up to help her. Then she was gone."

Who is this woman in pink? With so many stories, plus the background information gathered by the paranormal team, it doesn't seem that this is a phantom that can be dismissed as local lore embellished to near-mythic proportions. So if you are visiting Asheville, be sure to stop by the Grove Park Inn and book into room 545 for what may be a night to remember.

The Lodge on Lake Lure

Lake Lure, North Carolina

The Lodge on Lake Lure overlooks the Blue Ridge Mountains in western North Carolina with a spectacular view of the east end of the lake and all its wooded glory. Sitting high on the hillside, it is easy to see why in 1938 it was built by the State Highway Patrol as a retreat for highway patrolmen and their families. Surrounded by the natural beauty of the Appalachians, it is a place to relax, reflect and reconnect. And as many guests of the elegant, rambling inn will attest, it is also a place to get in touch with the spirit world.

"We have a very friendly and playful spirit here," says Jenny Chapman, the inn's administrative manager. "His presence has been felt quite often, sometimes just as a feeling that someone is standing over your shoulder."

The lodge's spectral guest is believed to be a former patrolman named George Penn. In 1937, the young officer died in a car crash during a high speed chase through the surrounding mountains in pursuit of two criminals. The highway patrol built the lodge the following year and, in honor of their fallen colleague, named it the George C. Penn Memorial Lodge. George knew the area well. He lived close to the nearby city of Asheville and was stationed between there and Lake Lure. Because he lived and died in the region, it is not surprising that his spirit took up residence in the haven built in his memory.

The highway patrol operated the lodge until 1968 and then sold it to the Town of Lake Lure. It changed hands several more times until it was bought from the IRS in the early 1980s and turned into a bed and breakfast.

Soon after the lodge opened to the public, stories surfaced of doors closing by themselves, drawers somehow becoming locked and objects disappearing and then turning up under beds. Previous owner Doris Nunn said in an interview for *Mid-Atlantic Country Magazine* that she got so tired of George's larking about, particularly his habit of slamming doors behind her as she cleaned, that she would chastise the spirit out loud.

In 1990, innkeepers Robin and Jack Stanier found that they too were host to the ghost. At a holiday dinner, their 38-year-old daughter Betsy apparently asked for a tangible sign that George was still present—and to everyone's astonishment she got one. A blue goblet rose off the buffet table and then fell to the floor in front of several witnesses. Many paranormal experts believe that it requires an inordinate amount of energy for spirits to manifest as an apparition or to pull off a task like picking up a glass, so perhaps George got the glass to move but then could not sustain it any longer.

The Staniers discovered that George preferred one room over the rest of the lodge. A guest staying in room 4 took Robin aside one day and whispered that she had seen an apparition of a man in her room. The woman explained that she woke up in the middle of the night to see someone walking in her room and told the person he was in the wrong room. She watched him go into the hallway and pace the halls. Her husband later told her that that was impossible because the door to the room was locked. A few weeks later as Robin told the story to other visitors, one guest asked if it had happened in room 4, and then admitted that the same thing had happened to her.

No one is sure why room 4 is the most haunted, given that George died prior to the lodge's construction and had no personal connection to any of the inn's 16 rooms. Could it be that four was his favorite number? Or, in some Asian cultures the number four is also a homonym for the word death, so perhaps George is letting people know in his ghostly way that he claims the room as is his quarters in the afterlife.

In 2000, current owner Giselle Hopke bought the lodge and began a long period of renovations. But as Jenny Chapman will tell you, not even the chaos of construction could deter the placid phantom. "We've been here eight years, and it has been a warm, fuzzy experience, with him standing over someone's shoulder or behind them," says Jenny. "We did a major renovation; a lot of things changed, but he still feels comfortable here, so he hung around."

Recently, a team of paranormal investigators came through with their equipment to check out the stories and see if they could get a lock on George. The report is confidential and Jenny is not free to share the details; however, the report does suggest that there is a spirit in the lodge and that all six people on the team had many individual inexplicable experiences.

Why does George stick around? Could it be that the young officer still considers himself a protector of the area he called home? Or perhaps he is just taking a *very* long holiday at the inn, having earned the time off for giving his life in the service of his community.

The Greystone Inn

Lake Toxaway, North Carolina

For a good haunting, head to the remote and magnificent man-made Lake Toxaway in the Appalachians of western North Carolina. There you may have the fortune of meeting Lucy Camp Armstrong Moltz at the inn that was once her private mansion. Lucy died in 1970, but she never gave up residence of the six-level manor she created on the edge of the lake as her own "little Switzerland." From actual sightings of Lucy to bizarre events such as fires lighting by themselves in fireplaces, there are many stories of ghostly events from employees and guests alike at the Greystone Inn.

Lake Toxaway didn't exist prior to the early 1900s. The area was pristine, rugged landscape nestled amid the mountains, with no roads to allow access. But entrepreneurs with a vision would change all that. Just as the Southern Railway developed its rail system, creating a vital link between the area and affluent travelers from the eastern cities, Pittsburgh entrepreneur E.H. Jennings dammed up the Toxaway River in 1902 to create a lake and an oasis for the wealthiest of society. Jennings also formed the Toxaway Company to create several high-end resorts around the newly formed lake. The Lake

Toxaway Inn opened in 1903 as a summer getaway for the rich and famous. The arrival of the railroad, creation of the lake and opening of the Toxaway Inn coincided to create the largest private lake enclave in the state, with 640 acres of land and 14 miles of shoreline. Soon after, the Fords, Firestones, Vanderbilts and Rockefellers signed the register to enjoy a private haven of serene splendor and solitude.

Among the many families who came to the Toxaway Inn were the Armstrongs of Savannah, Georgia. Lucy and George spent many summers there rejuvenating and relaxing in the crisp mountain air. Lucy fell in love with the area—it reminded her of Switzerland. She was quoted as saying, "I've been around the world twice, and I've found there's no place more beautiful or special than Lake Toxaway." The minute that land became available, she bought herself 40 acres. In 1915, Lucy brought her entourage of 11 servants and camped out on the property while she built her home.

In an unkind twist of fate, just one year after moving into her dream Swiss-style mansion, Lucy awakened to see the entire lakebed empty. Heavy rains had caused severe flooding throughout the area, and on August 13, 1916, the earthen dam broke; the lake drained overnight. Although Lucy's home and the Toxaway Inn survived, the damage destroyed the idyllic holiday destination. The inn lost its business, and after 30 years of standing empty it was torn down in 1948.

Undaunted, Lucy remained committed to the region and returned annually to her mountain getaway. She moved there permanently in 1924 after her first husband died. Six years later she married local lumber baron Carl Moltz. It took another three decades for the lake to be restored, and Lucy lived 10 years beyond that. She was 87 when she died.

The Moltz home nearly fell to bulldozers to make way for new condominiums, but residents of Lake Toxaway sought a court order and, in a dramatic last-minute rescue, managed to stop the demolition. Eventually, the 16,000-square-foot mansion became the Greystone Inn. Shortly after it opened in 1985, the stories of Lucy still pacing the floors began to surface. Former employees of Lucy Moltz remember her as a strict woman with high standards for the many people in her employ. Lucy ran a tight ship, so perhaps she continues her reign as matriarch even from the other side of the veil. Most of the paranormal activity takes place in the Presidential Suite, which was Lucy's library and her favorite room in the house.

In March 1999, Bob Smith stayed two nights in the room, and both evenings when he came back from dinner he found that someone had locked the deadbolt from the inside of the room. Other guests in the suite claim to have been kept awake through the night by the distinct creaking of someone walking on the wooden floor, but there is no one to be seen. In September 2008, Linda Brown was surprised to find a window in the suite open because it was the type that had to be hand-cranked open. She closed the window. Then the door opened. She closed the door, and the window opened again. Could it be that Lucy needed a breath of that fresh mountain air she so loved?

The best—and eeriest—story from the Presidential Suite occurred one fall as two bellmen were out gathering firewood. The back door to the suite opened, and an older couple dressed in unusual, somewhat dated clothing emerged walking arm in arm. They stopped to tell the bellmen that they were going up to dinner and would like to have a fire in the room when they returned. Dutifully, the bellmen each grabbed an armful of wood and walked around to the suite's front entrance, which faces out onto the lake. Because they had just seen the older couple leave, the bellmen assumed the room was empty and opened the door to carry the wood inside. To their surprise, they were met by a younger man in his robe who denied requesting any firewood. One of the bellmen quickly explained that it had been the older couple staying in the room who requested a fire. The man said there was no one else staying there. Later, when the bellmen were asked to describe the elderly couple, it became clear that they had seen Lucy and Carl Moltz.

Erin Connarn put together a short video documenting many of these inexplicable incidents at the hotel, including her own strange experience. She was working turn-down service and knocked on the door to the Moltz room. She heard a woman's voice say, "Who is it?" and replied, "Turn-down." The woman inside said, "Hold on just a minute." Erin waited, then knocked again: no answer. Thinking that was a little weird, she opened the door to find the room empty.

Visitor George Newberry stayed in the Moltz room in May 1998 and woke to a warm, cozy room—then he realized that someone had lit the gas fire early in the morning while he slept with the door locked. Apparently the former owner still tends to the comfort of the guests under her roof. There is no doubt that Lucy loved her house dearly.

Should you make the trek out to Lake Toxaway, there is nothing like it for charm and pampering—and the occasional phantom. Employees at the inn say that Lucy is a friendly ghost. In fact, many people come hoping to experience her spirit and leave disappointed. But there is always the golf, swimming, waterskiing, spa, gourmet food, scenery and hiking to give visitors something to remember.

The Blennerhassett Hotel

Parkersburg, West Virginia

How ironic that a deluxe hotel from the *Gaslight* era should house a considerable roster of ghosts. It was in the classic 1944 motion picture *Gaslight* that Ingrid Bergman nearly lost her mind hearing footsteps in the attic and seeing the gaslights dim before her eyes. Events at the Blennerhassett Hotel in Parkersburg, West Viginia, are not nearly so sinister but do have some guests wondering if their mind is playing tricks on them.

Just ask Becky Sheehy. She works throughout the hotel bartending and serving, and in her three and a half years on staff she has an impressive list of eerie experiences. "When I started I had heard rumors that it was haunted, and I had not decided whether or not to believe any of it," she says. "But I've had some pretty scary experiences. Yes! The hotel is haunted!"

Becky's first inexplicable incident happened soon after she started working at the hotel. She was on her way downstairs to the basement when she saw a little boy peek around the corner at her and then run off. "He was seven or eight years old. His hair was kind of tousled and brown. From the one shoulder I saw as he looked around the corner it appeared he was wearing suspenders, and I thought, is there a wedding going on?"

Becky followed the boy, worried that there was an unsupervised youngster running around the basement. She was not far behind him, but when she went around the corner there was no one there. "The hall doesn't go anywhere, it's a dead end. So I thought he must have ducked into one of the restrooms," Becky explains. "I checked out both the men's and ladies' restrooms, but they were empty." She tried to shrug it off, but the boy had seemed so solid. "He didn't look like a ghost. I'm more the type who wants to disprove it, but I saw it. I know it happened."

When Becky told other people about the boy, she learned that there are quite a few little ghost children running around the Blennerhassett. There was a chef who regularly saw and heard the phantom half-pints running around the kitchen. And about three years ago, guest services manager Dorinda Conner was working the front desk when two middle-aged women came to check in because they were looking for ghost experiences. Dorinda recalls, "They said they like to stay at historic haunted hotels and asked me what stories I knew." She shared a few of the better known stories but failed to mention the ghostly brood.

The next morning, Dorinda was at the front desk again as the women checked out. When she asked about their stay, one of the ladies said, "Go ahead and tell her." Expecting news of bad service, Dorinda was surprised at the tale they told. One of the women awoke in the middle of the night sensing that somebody was in her room. She tried to doze off again, but then she heard some children laughing and felt someone tickling the bottom of her feet.

A housekeeper working on the fourth floor told Dorinda of a strange encounter with the spectral children. While cleaning the bathroom she got a feeling that there was somebody in the room, but when she turned around the room was empty. She continued cleaning but heard a strange noise, like giggling. When she came out of the bathroom she saw two impressions in the foam bench at the foot of the bed. As the housekeeper realized what she was seeing, the indentations raised back up. She swore the marks were the size of children's feet, as if they were standing on the bench and then jumped off. Dorinda went to the bench to investigate but could find nothing amiss with the foam or anything that might make those marks.

Also on the fourth floor, back during the hotel's renovation process, Dorinda had an odd incident occur during a meeting with an interior designer. "We went to a fourth-floor room to see how it had been done and to talk about what to do on the third floor. As we walked in I saw that the bedroom window and the bathroom shutters were wide open. I shut the window and shutters, and I remember I had laid my pad of paper down on a table next to the bed."

The next day Dorinda followed up with the housekeeper to remind her to be more careful about closing windows. But the employee firmly denied leaving anything open. "She said the windows were open when she went in to clean. It was the first thing she noticed, and she shut them." The housekeeper confirmed that she shut the window in the bedroom and the shutters in the bathroom. "The room had not been booked that night, so I went in to check with the housekeeping manager and the windows were still shut. But where I had laid my pad of paper there was a strange puddle of water, plus an odd puddle on the bathroom floor. I know it wasn't there before because my paper would have been wet," says Dorinda.

A family of four staying at the hotel over Christmas 2007 shared their ghost child experience with Becky Sheehy. The mother and son had gone out, and the father and daughter remained behind at the hotel. The father went downstairs to smoke, and while he was gone, his daughter watched two little boys running around playing in the room until they eventually ran out—*through* the door. "It freaked her out quite a bit," says Becky, who pointed out that that had occurred on the fifth floor, adding, "It's very rare to hear stories from there."

Becky's next experience took place about six months into her tenure. "I was helping some of the girls do room service and was making a delivery to the fourth floor. I got off the elevator, and as I walked down the hallway I felt a distinct shove to the point where I stumbled." Luckily there were no drinks on her tray. Becky turned to see who had pushed her, but she was alone. "Then I smelled the cigar smoke. So now I'm thinking, okay, that's weird. It creeped me out a bit. This was in the daytime too."

Becky was not the only person to get a shove. One day a visibly shaken housekeeper told Dorinda Conner that she had been going into a room on the second floor to clean it, and the minute she put the key in the lock and turned it she felt someone grab her forcefully by both shoulders and push her into the room. Thinking it was someone with whom she worked, the housekeeper whipped around and said, "Michael!" But no one was in the hall. There was nowhere to hide, either.

Most of the stories of the cigar-smoking man that haunts the hotel come from the second floor, but the spirit behind the pungent smoke roams throughout the Blennerhassett. After all, he built it. Colonel William N. Chancellor designed and built the elegant hotel at the juncture of Fourth and Market streets at the height of the oil and gas boom of the late 1800s. The wealthy oilman spared no expense for his showcase property, with 50 guestrooms built around a central staircase, lavish interiors, a library and an atrium. Colonel Chancellor named his hotel after Harman and Margaret Blennerhassett, early settlers to the area.

Despite its prominence when it opened in 1889 the hotel gradually lost its shine, and by the early 1980s it was on a list of properties to face a wrecking ball. Saved by a massive restoration effort, the hotel became a historic site and has risen in stature to again be a top place to stay in the mid–Ohio Valley. Perhaps the colonel felt compelled to oversee the renovations done to his pride and joy, but whatever the reason, William Chancellor is well known as a permanent resident at the Blennerhassett.

Not only is Colonel Chancellor seen in the halls on the second floor where Becky Sheehy met him, but he is also known to visit guests in their rooms. In summer 2008, a female guest came down to the bar in sweat pants and t-shirt, visibly shaking. She asked Becky for a glass of wine. Becky naturally asked her what was wrong. "You'll think I'm crazy," she told Becky. She had gone bed early, around 9 PM, Becky says, "then she told me, 'I awakened to a man sitting on the end of my bed smoking a cigar. I screamed, turned on the light and he was gone.'" The guest had been staying on the fourth floor. "She has stayed since but sleeps with the lights on," says Becky.

Other guests report smelling the cigar smoke or seeing smoke hanging in the air, which is noteworthy in West Virginia because smoking in public buildings is prohibited. Apparently William Chancellor has not kept up with the law.

He has, however, kept up with his reading; the other place he visits frequently is his library. Every so often, a book is pulled out on the shelf, sometimes so far that it drops to the floor, when no one is nearby. One book in particular gets pulled out or thrown to the floor. "It's an old book," says Becky, "but it is not a particularly interesting book. It is about engineering."

Recently, two guests relaxing in the library discovered this phenomenon with the help of their two dogs. As they sat reading, one dog lay under the table while the other was close to the doors. All of a sudden both jumped up at the same time, ran to the corner and began barking while looking up. Becky had joined the guests to chat with them and saw what had the dogs so worked up. "Sure enough, that book was pulled out. Then the lady said, 'That's funny. The same thing happened last night.'"

On another occasion, Becky heard books hitting the floor. The library was empty. She was standing at the front desk when she suddenly heard *thud, thud, thud*. Inside the library, she saw several books tossed onto the floor. "People probably think I'm crazy, but I will say out loud things like 'that's enough,'" she says of events like that one.

On a local Fox News blog site, a Blennerhassett guest posted his library experience on February 9, 2009. Bruce

Layman wrote that while typing on his laptop, he heard "the sound of a newspaper being rustled, then being opened up, and then—section by section—being dropped to the floor." It was a brief incident to which he gave almost no thought until he realized that "no one had entered the library...and upon turning around saw no newspaper on the floor and most importantly, NO ONE behind me."

In addition to the colonel and the children, there are other spirits at the hotel. One little boy staying on the third floor ran down one night very afraid and asking, "Are there g-g-ghosts in the hotel?" He said the reason for his question was that he was coming down to go to the coffee shop, and as he left his room he saw a lady get on the elevator. He ran to catch it, not wanting to wait for the next one, and when he got on the lady was gone. Becky says that story is becoming a common one. "Many people are reporting that they see an older woman, plainly dressed, get on the elevator, but when they get there, she is gone. No one knows who she might be."

Another guest was a little spooked by his encounter with the hotel's paranormal entities. The man was sleeping on the fifth floor when he woke to the sound of his door slamming shut. He sat up and saw a woman and little girl walking through the room. He told them, "You're in the wrong room!" When he turned on the lights, they disappeared before his eyes. "He checked out as soon as he could get out, about 5 AM," chuckles Becky.

A pair of sisters who meet regularly at the hotel as a halfway point were shocked during one recent visit to discover that they were not the sole occupants of their room. They reported being awakened at 6:37 AM by their smoke detector beeping three times. One sister looked at the other and asked, "Did you hear that?" When her sister replied that she had, the first then asked, "Okay, do you *see* that in the bathroom?" Both sisters couldn't believe their eyes. A woman with long, dark hair stood there laughing at them and then faded away.

Dorinda Conner has been on the receiving end of a lot of stories, but, she says, "I've only experienced one thing personally myself, and I don't know whether I believe in ghosts or not. Until I actually see an apparition or something, I'm not sure." However, she admits that there is not an obvious explanation for the event that happened to her about five years ago.

She was the front office manager at the time and arrived at 7 AM to her basement office in the administrative area. "I worked in a little area away from everyone else. I was just getting started, turning on my computer, and had only been there 10 minutes or so. I kept hearing a noise and wasn't sure what it was, but it got louder and louder. Then I realized it was a woman crying."

Dorinda's office was next to the archival storage area, and her first thought was that "someone was back there having a bad day and needed to get away." When the crying persisted she investigated, but no one was there. "I returned to my desk thinking I was hearing things." Dorinda no sooner sat down than the sound started again, a crescendo from very low weeping to heavy sobbing. Compelled to find the unhappy person, she got up again to search the area. "As I got up, I realized another person had come into work. We met in the middle of the office and we both said, "Do you hear that?"

After checking the ballroom above the office and the rooms nearby, they determined that no one was there. "It wasn't even 7:30 yet," says Dorinda. "The other woman told me she had heard it before, but always very early before anyone else came in. She was glad someone else had finally heard it." It only happened the one time for Dorinda, and to this day she is not sure what she heard or what to make of it.

Dozens of incidents with the elevators suggest that some playful spirit likes to mess with the guests. Becky says, "It even happened to me a couple of weeks ago. It shook, the lights for all the buttons were flashing on and off, and the doors wouldn't close properly." The elevators have been checked, and nothing turned up to cause the malfunctions. Could it be that the vanishing lady people see is playing ghostly games? Or is the colonel riding the elevators to explore his hotel and check in on the guests?

Some other spirit certainly wanted to get Becky's attention—and it was with a bar full of people watching. Within six months of starting as a bartender, Becky was mixing drinks near the shelves in front of the ice bins. Suddenly two wine glasses flew off another shelf, hit her in the leg and smashed to the ground. "At first I thought maybe the shelf had been overstocked and they had just slipped off—but there were only five or six more glasses up there. And then I realized the glasses flew five feet sideways." Other witnesses still talk about it as proof that the Blennerhassett is haunted. As if, with the litany of stories that emerge almost daily, anyone could doubt it.

Most of the stories carry with them a benign energy. In most instances it seems that the spirits are not even aware of their surroundings. But there are some signs of spirit life with which Becky does not feel entirely comfortable. "I didn't feel concerned about all the ghosts until last week," she says.

The dining room is the occasional setting for a certain paranormal phenomenon that has been experienced by some staff members. In preparing to close up for the night, they blow out all the candles. Often they leave for some reason, and when they return the candles are relit. It happened several times to Becky and didn't bother her at all. "Last week, however, I heard my name called. I distinctly heard one of the bellmen yell for me. I answered, 'What?' He didn't answer me. So I went to front desk and asked if Ryan had just called for me." The front desk person told Becky that Ryan left some time earlier. Becky then asked if anyone else was there. She was told no. Then she turned around, and all the candles on the right side of the room were relit. "It scared me that the voice mimicked the sound of another employee," she says. "Then I felt a lot of negative energy in there. I felt like I was being watched." Rather than let it phase her, Becky intends to let the spirit know she is not worried or leaving.

Meanwhile, the Blennerhassett ghosts keep life interesting. The hotel certainly deserves its status as a National Historic Landmark and probably qualifies as one of the most haunted buildings in the country. So for those of you who see, hear or smell things that seem strange, it may not be your mind playing tricks but rather one of the many mischievous spirits that stay there.

The Green Park Inn

Blowing Rock, North Carolina

When a hotel has enough ghosts to host paranormal conferences, the odds are it is steeped in supernatural lore. The Green Park Inn certainly has a reputation for having an abundance of specters. Thriller author Scott Nicholson considers it to be "the most haunted hotel in the Blue Ridge Mountains."

From its lofty perch at 4300 feet above sea level on the Eastern Continental Divide, the sprawling green and white inn sits on the former site of a Civil War stockade. George Kirk and his motley gang of scoundrels known as Kirk's Raiders used to travel through on their way to Ohio, leaving bloodshed and misery in their wake. In 1882, Major George Washington Finley Harper, formerly of the Confederate Army, teamed with a group of Lenoir, North Carolina, businessmen to build the Green Park Inn, with a vision of creating a summer getaway for those who could afford it.

And the wealthy came in droves to sit on the breezy verandas in white wicker chaise lounges and talk about what the rest of the world must be doing to cope with the oppressive summer heat. Mind you, those who stayed at the inn had an adventurous spirit; to get there required traveling by horseback up a precipitous mountain trail. Eventually investors built a toll road to enable easier passage, and then the guest list read like that of an inaugural dinner, with names such as Herbert Hoover, Eleanor Roosevelt, Calvin Coolidge and Margaret Mitchell. In its isolation,

Green Park eventually became a town with its own post office, dairy farm, casino and golf course. The inn was the first hotel in the state to have electric lights.

But how does a hotel get so many spirits? It turns out that over the 127 years of providing a place for people to rest their head, some of the guests left feet first. There are a few deaths on the hotel's records, and as a result, some of the rooms come with the added bonus of supernatural activity. As time passed, the list of experiences grew to the point that the hotel now keeps a "ghost registry" at the front desk to keep track of the all the eerie happenings.

Room 318 is the most famous of their haunted rooms; it is where Laurel Green hung herself in her bridal gown when her fiancé left her at the church and never returned. The jilted woman is not a happy entity, according to Cassandra Reed, acting manager and sales director of the inn. "She was believed to be just 18 years old and was essentially left at the altar," says Cassandra.

Guests often feel the bride's presence, and some of them say that they have the strong sensation of someone standing next to them. Many guests claim to have actually seen an apparition of a woman walking up and down the halls at night. From the street, some people have seen a woman in the window of the room when the room is empty.

The bride may have company, too. There have been several reports of smelling pipe smoke in the room, "and that's only allowed in the bar," says Cassandra. "The belief is that the guilty groom comes around searching for Laurel."

One of Cassandra's favorite accounts recorded in the ghost registry for room 318 came from a woman who woke at 3:30 AM to the sound of giggling. The woman got up and followed the voice to the bathroom, but the sound stopped. Since she was there she decided to use the toilet, and as she washed her hands afterward, she felt a cool breeze pass across her face. When she turned off the water to dry her hands, the woman felt water on her face. She dried it off with a towel, but it happened again as she left the room. She woke her husband, who said that he had just dreamed of a beautiful lady in the bathroom with a wash pan and that water was pouring onto the floor. The couple returned to the bathroom and were astonished to see a puddle on the floor and a ring that looked like someone had had a pan sitting there.

Other rooms listed as haunted are 131, 210, 218, 327, 332 and 333. Of rooms 210 and 327, Cassandra has this to say: "I hate those rooms. Room 327 was the caretaker's room. To me it's like an overwhelming feeling of sadness or loneliness. It just feels empty—I know that something happened there." No deaths are recorded in room 327, but the hotel is still trying to track down an accurate history of events over the years.

Other people have also felt uneasy in room 327, some even feeling an evil presence. One time during a historical tour, 15 tourists jammed into the tiny space, and suddenly the television started turning itself on and off. Then the radio in the room did the same thing. It turns out that that's a good way to clear out a room, because the group fled. Another guest reported that when her children got into the room, they started screaming and ran out for no apparent reason. They ultimately had to change rooms.

As for room 210, Cassandra says, "It freaks me out the most. I can't breathe right in that room." She compares the feeling to someone sitting on her chest. "I took my daughter up without saying anything, and she says, 'Mom, I can't breathe right, it feels bad here.'" Cassandra wonders if someone was smothered in there. Some guests have reported seeing children around the ages of 11 and 13 in the room. Others report more benign experiences in the second-floor room, such as hearing children laughing. Could it be that some rooms contain the energy of more than one spirit or experience? That might explain the huge variance in what people sense.

On the third floor, people hear children playing in the hall, laughing and running. "That area used to be the nursery for kids way back when," says Cassandra. "It's a happy energy." But in the same area, rooms 332 and 333 are listed on the registry by guests who experienced bad or ill feelings. Others reported feeling closed in or smothered.

Down in the kitchen, one of the few employee ghosts keeps staff on their toes. A chef for the inn died of a heart attack during the late 1950s or 1960s. Many of the workers have seen something move out of the corner of their eye or claim that objects were moved.

The newest room to have paranormal activity is on the first floor. "Room 131," states Cassandra. "It has been four years since there was a suicide in there, and that room is now becoming extremely active." Reports are vague so far, but some guests have reported feeling a cold breeze pass through them and a general sense of unease in the room.

So what does a hotel do when it has so much unseen and unexplainable action? Invite a lot of people who specialize in the paranormal and give them free run of the place, according to Cassandra. In November 2008, around 100 ghost hunters came to the Green Park Inn's first paranormal conference for three days of panels, presentations and "wall to wall ghost hunting."

Joe Wright of Paranormal Scene Investigators says that over the course of the weekend "a lot of paranormal activity was observed and recorded." PSI investigator April Isaac recorded an electronic voice phenomenon (EVP) on November 22, 2008: in response to her question, "Do you mind if we take your picture?" a disembodied voice says, "No pictures." Joe says his role was more to assist with the conference than to investigate, adding that it wasn't an ideal time to gather material because of the large number of people moving around and making noise. Even so, he and his wife had an experience in their room. "My wife felt something crawling up the bottom of the bed to the center at about 2 AM. She said it felt like a small child that crawls in between you."

Some groups recorded EVPs that were believed to be voices from beyond the grave. Others gathered evidence of cold spots and strange fluctuations in electromagnetic fields. One team working with a medium felt it communicated with the spirit of a little girl. Overall, attendees left feeling sure that the Green Park Inn is a paranormal hub of activity, and Cassandra says that they will host an annual paranormal conference every November.

So even if you tend to be in the "show me and I'll believe it" camp, a visit to Blowing Rock's Green Park Inn might tip the scales on the side of "maybe there's more here than meets the eye."

The Chester Inn and Other Haunts

Jonesborough, Tennessee

The town of Jonesborough seems too small and serene to accommodate such a sprawling spectral history. It was listed by the Travel Channel in a recent documentary as one of the top 10 haunted towns in America. There is but one street running through from one end to the other—the second oldest wagon road in the state. This town is part of the original western frontier. It is like a living museum; most of the buildings on either side of Main Street have that distinctive symmetry of Federal-period architecture. Maybe that's why the ghosts like staying there; it still feels like home.

In the early 1770s, this part of northeastern Tennessee was part of North Carolina and was being settled by audacious adventurers who defied the British ban on immigration past the Appalachians. Jonesborough is the oldest town in Tennessee. It was established in 1779, 17 years before Tennessee became a state. The town's name came from legislator Willie Jones, who supported North Carolina's westward expansion over the Appalachian Mountains. In 1780, the first tract of 100 acres, divided into one-acre lots, went up for sale at $75 each. They were so popular that they had to be awarded by lottery.

The region became part of Tennessee Territory in 1796. As a quick aside, the town's audacity never waned. It was the heart of the abolitionist movement within states that would join the Confederacy in the Civil War. Elihu Embree printed *The Emancipator* in 1820 in Jonesborough—the first American periodical to be dedicated exclusively to the issue of the abolition of slavery. And although Tennessee later joined the Confederacy, most East Tennesseans leaned in favor of the Union.

In a small town, it is easy to track down the ghosts. The Chester Inn and the Eureka Inn are the two most haunted buildings in the town, as documented by ongoing research conducted by the Alternate Realities Center. The ARC was founded in 1994 by international director Stacey Allen McGee, who took several training programs to become a certified ghost hunter. "It seems like the work is never done. On our tours we are always gathering information," stresses Stacey. "It is impossible to overstate how active this town and the surrounding region is."

The streets of the town are extremely lively in terms of paranormal goings-on. People on the ghost tours are touched by unseen hands on shoulders, arms or legs, they feel hands run through their hair, and the street lamps go on and off. Stacey states, "This is real substantial stuff, physical manifestations." There are also signs that people are standing close to a ghost: "They have shortness of breath, feel clothing tugged on, have cold chills…" It may be easier to find a place in town that is *not* haunted than to list all the ghosts of Jonesborough. "This is typical of most of the western frontier towns that we tour."

Stacey is a direct descendant of the Tipton family, who were some of the first settlers in the area. Colonel John Tipton, Stacey's sixth great-uncle, bargained with the Cherokee for a tract of land near Jonesborough in

Washington County, where the late-1700s farmstead that he built is preserved by the state as a historic site to this day. "It's also very haunted," laughs Stacey, who runs walking ghost tours under the name of Appalachian GhostWalks through many towns in Tennessee. "What better way to tour the area than to have a ghost tour run by a blood relative?"

Stacey has committed most of his adult life to research of the paranormal. His organization has done 16 years of research in Tennessee, from Knoxville to Jonesborough and all the way north to Virgina, discovering some amazing details of the region's ghosts along the way. "Through the art of dowsing we have determined the number of spirits, the male to female ratios and have helped to resolve issues— helped spirits move on," says Stacey. "It helps our students— because we teach a course on dowsing—to look at the afterlife in a positive way."

The Chester Inn

The Chester Inn, the first boarding house and second oldest building in Jonesborough, is haunted by multiple ghosts. Dr. William P. Chester of Berlin, Pennsylvania, built the inn to serve the stage coach line in 1797, and over time enlarged the structure so it could take in more guests. It was a popular resting place for many famous travelers, including President Andrew Jackson, who even held a reception for his friends out on the front porch during the summer of 1832, the year he was re-elected; it is also rumored that Andrew Jackson was threatened with tar and feathering at the Chester Inn.

The inn is now owned by the State of Tennessee as a designated historic site, and the state leases the space to the

National Storytelling Association, which hosts a national festival for storytelling every October. The inn is also part museum and has two rooms open for public touring. One staff member with the storytelling association says she has not seen anything remotely ghost-like but admits that ghosts do make good stories to add to the collection.

Stacey maintains that the inn is actively haunted. "Our guests have seen visions of ghosts. We've had unbelievable photographs on the porches." He holds tight to the details of what specters have been seen, as that is part of his tour. But he did share this experience: on a March 2009 tour, everyone in the group watched in amazement as the lights sputtered on and off in the inn when it was empty. "We've checked into the possibility of faulty wiring," says Stacey, but that was ruled out as a cause of the flickering lights. "We also see curtains pulled back by unseen hands, and we checked to see if there's a vent that could be blowing on them, but nothing—in fact, the windows are sealed shut by paint."

The Eureka Inn

The Eureka Inn also has a myriad of ghosts. "According to our research it's the most haunted place in Jonesborough," says Stacey enthusiastically. "You can look up at the porch and watch all the chairs move when there's not a breath of wind."

The third oldest building was almost the second oldest; it was built across the street from the Chester Inn just a few months later. Robert and Harriet Mitchell bought lot 19 from the town in the spring of 1797 and built a home on the corner of First Avenue and Main Street. In 1851, William Henry Maxwell became the new owner and expanded the home with a two-story addition.

At the turn of the century, Peter Miller and his wife Harriet bought the building with a vision of completely revamping it and creating a hotel. They built two-story additions on either end of the original home, added three big porches and installed a new metal roof, then opened for business as the Eureka Inn. For 60 years the inn passed through various owners and names. There was a three-decade period from the 1960s to the 1990s where neglect and disrepair nearly spelled the end of the structure, but a group of Jonesborough business people bought the property in 1997; three years and $2.5 million later, the refurbished hotel opened once again under its original name.

With so much history, it is not all that unexpected that there are many ghosts that still hang out on the porch and wander the halls after the guests have turned in for the night. "There are several male and female spirits in the Eureka," says Stacey McGee, reluctant to part with details that he gives out on his tours.

Haunt Master's Club investigator Angela Miles agrees with Stacey's assessment. She was part of a seven-person team to investigate the Eureka in January 2009. The group recorded several electronic voice phenomena (EVPs), though what was captured digitally did not in any way connect to the questions asked. One recording is a voice saying "horse shoe." Angela and another investigator also picked up the strong scent of lilac while in one of the upstairs bedrooms. Although none of the evidence gathered led the group to any conclusions about what spirits might linger there, Angela had an experience of her own that "scared the bejeebies" out of her.

As a sensitive, when Angela investigates she does an initial scan to get a feeling for the place, then does another check during the investigation to see if that feeling chan-ges. She didn't have the chance when the team first arrived at the Eureka Inn. "We were downstairs setting up the equipment and doing some base readings to get temper-atures and the like," she explains, "and then the guys went upstairs to look around."

Angela followed but stopped at the bottom of the stairs to get a sense of the place. "I heard a downstairs door to one of the bedrooms open plain as day, and then I heard soft footsteps coming this way. When they got to the opening of the reception area I could still hear them, but there was no person," says Angela.

All of a sudden, the footsteps came straight toward her; she heard them pounding the floor, running right at her. "They got to within three feet of me, and that's when I ran up the stairs. I was definitely being charged by some-thing, and though it wasn't necessarily negative, it was unexpected. It spooked me." The weight of the footsteps led Angela to believe it was either a man or a heavy-set woman. Although they did not capture the sound on audio, nothing can convince her that it didn't happen or that the Eureka Inn doesn't have **ghosts**.

Innkeeper Maria Bledsoe dismisses the notion of ghosts at the hotel, despite the many investigations that have taken place. "If we do have ghosts, then they are scared of me because they know I would charge them to stay here," she says with a laugh. "I don't think we have any."

One of the very public ghosts in the town is that of former president Andrew Jackson, who spent many years in the area and professed a fondness for the town. There are many accounts of people seeing Jackson's apparition walking down

Main Street toward the old courthouse. People who spot the president note that anyone walking on the same side of the street doesn't seem to notice him.

Jonesborough resident Sue Henley (see her story on page 16) had a remarkable experience one summer evening a few years ago while out walking past the Eureka Inn with her husband and some friends. "It was about five years ago," recalls Sue, "and a group of us went out walking. We were strolling right by the Eureka when we saw a man on the porch in a long, old-fashioned black topcoat that went all the way down to his shoes, heavy black boots, and a big stovepipe hat on. We all saw it. This was July, and I thought it strange that someone was in heavy winter clothes." Then Sue and her friends watched as the unusually dressed fellow stepped off the curb in front of them and began walking down the block; he even turned to look over his shoulder at the astonished group. "My husband and another friend followed him, but no matter how fast they went, they couldn't catch up. The man went down street about two blocks, into a parking lot and just disappeared."

To this day Sue is convinced that she saw a supernatural spirit. "I think it was Andrew Jackson," she says. "I can't imagine what else it could be. We checked with the hotel and asked if there was any actor staying there that would be dressed like that, and they said no."

Christopher Taylor House

The oldest city in the state of Tennessee still has one of the oldest houses built in the area. It is one of the few remaining examples of 18th-century pioneer architecture. But the address for the Christopher Taylor House is different than when it was first built. Back in 1788 when Major Taylor initially constructed his two-story log cabin, he situated the house about two miles out of town. From there the North Carolina native could do his job of protecting the locals from Indian attack and also raise his brood of 10 children. He also hosted the famous self-taught lawyer and future president, Andrew Jackson—Jackson lived on and off in Taylor's home for several months while he waited for enough travelers to fill a caravan before leaving to work as a public prosecutor in the Cumberland (now Nashville).

Not quite 200 years later, in 1974, the cabin was moved to 124 West Main Street to be restored as a historic site. It is not clear if the seventh president of the United States haunted the log home on its original site, but it soon became obvious that Andrew Jackson followed the trail to the new location. "The first sightings of Jackson began the year the house was moved," cites Stacey McGee. Jackson died in 1845, but his ghost appears at the Christopher Taylor House from time to time. Local legend has it that his figure appears to walk up to the front door and then passes through into the building. Obviously his familiarity with the house continues even in the afterlife.

Stacey looked into Jackson's history a little further and says no one has ever seen his ghost at his own homestead or where he died. "Ghosts don't always haunt where they die," says Stacey, "but they haunt where they were happiest."

6
Mountainside Haunts

Mamie Thurman's Ghost

Logan, West Virginia

Whoever killed young Mamie Thurman in the summer of 1932 *really* wanted her dead. Her mutilated body had been shot twice in the head, her throat was cut from ear to ear and her neck was broken. Although two men were arrested, a trial ensued and one man served time for the horrible crime, the murder remains an unsolved mystery. And ironically, the murder victim defied her brutal killer's wish to see the end of her because Mamie's ghost continues to roam the hills of Logan, West Virginia, in search of an elusive thing called justice.

Mamie's death ignited the small town of Logan. How could it not? Intrigue, adultery and jealousy pierced the heart of the Bible belt. On June 23, 1932, the *Charleston Gazette* proclaimed, "Body of Comely Logan Woman Found, Throat Cut, Bullets in Brain." That headline would create a sensation any day.

Much has been written about this decades-old murder. The story unfolds as follows. A deaf-mute boy named Garland Davis was out picking berries on No. 22 Mountain when he discovered Mamie's body, unceremoniously dumped in a ditch on the side of the road. She wore a blue polka-dot dress and had one shoe on. She still wore her diamond rings and expensive watch, and a purse with $10 in it lay nearby; robbery was not the motive. An autopsy revealed two close-range bullet wounds from a .38 caliber gun. The slash to her throat cut right through her trachea, carotid artery and jugular vein. There was bruising to her right eye. And her spine had been snapped at the second cervical vertebrae.

The question on everyone's lips was, who would want to kill the attractive brunette, a police officer's wife known throughout the community as socially active and a good church member?

As if Mamie's murder wasn't shocking enough, the townspeople reeled at the news that, late on the same day Mamie's body was found, police arrested a prominent city official and his black handyman in connection with the killing. Harry Robertson, banker, president of the city council and library treasurer, was taken into custody along with Clarence Stephenson, who worked for Robertson doing odd jobs and caring for his employer's hunting dogs.

On the day of Mamie's funeral, police searched Robertson's home and found bloody rags in the basement, spots of blood on the floor, a hole in the wall that appeared to be from a bullet, and a razor stained with blood. In Robertson's Ford sedan, the same one he used for hunting, they found bloodstains under the floor mats (which were determined to be human blood). Witnesses came forward saying they saw a black man driving the car up the No. 22 Mountain road the night Mamie died.

Rumors of an illicit affair-gone-bad were confirmed during Robertson's indictment hearing, and the seamy underside of Logan's elite was exposed. He testified before a Grand Jury that he belonged to a "key club"—a secret group of Logan's wealthier citizens who had keys to a rented room in which they could rendezvous with their lovers. Robertson admitted to carrying on an affair with Mamie for more than two years, but in a move likely meant to cast doubt on his position as sole murder suspect, Robertson claimed to have a list of 16 other men with whom Mamie kept acquaintance. He claimed that he continued his affair with Mamie even though she refused to give up her dalliances with the other men. Robertson said Clarence Stephenson often acted as a go-between for his meetings with Mamie, picking her up and driving her to the appointed meeting place.

Clarence Stephenson said little, refusing to implicate Robertson but claiming his own innocence. The inquiry lasted four days. Ultimately—it was the 1930s in the South—the Grand Jury set Robertson free. Stephenson went to trial, was found guilty and was sent to the Moundsville Penitentiary. He died in prison in 1942 of cancer, still proclaiming he had not harmed Mamie Thurman.

So what of the other prominent businessmen with whom Mamie carried on her adulterous affairs? Or Mamie's husband Jack, the cuckolded community police officer? Or even Harry's wife, who admitted she hated Mamie? The crime raised a lot of questions and did not ever result in a conviction that locals considered to be valid. Many people felt that Stephenson took the fall for the killer, whether it was Robertson or some other member of Logan's elite society.

It would seem that Mamie was unhappy with how the courts handled her death as well. It wasn't long after the case was considered closed that stories started to surface about ghostly sightings and weird happenings on the mountain. People claimed to see the figure of a woman in a polka-dot dress walking along the road near where Mamie's body was so callously discarded. Others tell a tale that sounds like an old urban legend, of drivers offering a lift to a woman who appeared to want a ride into town, only to have her disappear before leaving the mountain. Bus drivers who traveled the route from Holden to a town on the other side of the mountain claimed to pick up a woman in a remote stretch of the road late at night, but when they arrived at the town her seat was always empty.

On a website dedicated to solving Mamie's murder, this posting suggests people still have strange encounters on No. 22 Mountain. Posted by wv171: "This is a very true story and mystery... I used to work up on top and other side of 22 Mountain RD traveled it daily... This not the place to discuss it. But I bet there are way into the hundreds to maybe thousands people that swear they seen her ghost... You travel that RD to work 6 days a week for years you will become a believer too."

Most of the people who were directly connected to the event are now dead. And in a surprising twist, many of the court records and other key documents connected to the trial have disappeared. So if Mamie continues to roam the mountain, a lost soul in search of justice and closure, she may be around for a long time to come.

Strangely, no one is actually sure where Mamie is buried. Her remains were on record as being buried at Logan Memorial Park in McConnell. However, when a reporter researching her story in the 1980s tried to find her grave, he could not locate it. The funeral home has documents showing $35 was paid to move her body to a town in Kentucky, but the cemetery there has no record to show she was re-interred. Mamie's remains, like her spirit, seem to be in limbo.

If there's any peace to be found for her, it may come from the fact that even after all these years, there are still people trying to piece together what really happened on that night in June 1932, and the truth may surface yet.

Uncle Nick Grindstaff's Grave

Iron Mountain, Tennessee

Along the Appalachian Trail on Iron Mountain in the land between Tennessee and North Carolina, there is a stone monument bearing one of the world's most eloquent epitaphs. The sparse words carved into a chimney-shaped grave marker between Shady Valley and Stoney Creek are a poetic summation of the life of a hermit named Uncle Nick Grindstaff:

Lived alone.

Suffered alone.

Died alone.

That poignant description of one man's life sits at the base of an eight-foot marker built from local stone and embedded with shards from Uncle Nick's unusual life. High atop the windy ridge, three miles from the nearest road, the spirits that lived and died there still swirl among the scrubby pines and hemlock groves.

There are few concrete details of the life of Uncle Nick Grindstaff aside from the dates of his birth—December 26, 1851—and his death—July 22, 1923. But there is enough information around which to weave a sad tale of a man who felt forsaken by the world and so chose to abandon society.

Tragedy followed Nick Grindstaff through life. By the age of three, his mother, Mary Heaton Grindstaff, and his father Isaac were dead. Orphaned with three siblings, Nick lived with relatives until he turned 21, and then he became a landowner as his parents' farm was split equally between the four children. Nick built a house and tried his hand at farming, but he had an adventurer's heart, so, after five years behind a till, he sold his farm and traveled west in search of gold.

On the California coast, it seemed Nick might enjoy a bright, gold-tinged future. He met a young woman, fell in love and married her. But the glory days faded fast; Nick's young wife died. Bereft, he packed up his gold and headed back to Johnson County. There are different versions of what happened next. One story says that somewhere along the way, Nick stopped by a saloon and allowed himself to be enticed into a back room by a woman of dubious repute whose partner robbed Grindstaff of his gold. Another story—quite different—suggests that Nick turned to the bottle for comfort and drank himself into both despair and a big financial hole.

Either way, he ended up back in his birthplace destitute and derelict. He bought a parcel of land on top of Iron Mountain and secluded himself there with only his dog Panter, a steer and a rattlesnake for company. The hermit Grindstaff did venture down the mountain twice a year to visit the Shady Valley general store and stock up on provisions, but otherwise, he wanted no contact with the world that had brought him only pain and heartache.

It happened that Baxter McEwen checked on Nick one July day in 1923 and found the 72-year-old hermit dead inside his shack. Nick's dog had remained by his side for several days to protect him. Some stories suggest that the dog had to be killed in order for people to come and collect the corpse, and that the dog was buried alongside its master. Other versions say Panter merely had to be tied to a tree before men could carry out the body. Nick's funeral on Iron Mountain drew a large crowd of 200 people, which is surprising given his almost lifelong shunning of society. Perhaps people were curious to finally see where this fellow of their community had sequestered himself. It didn't take long for stories to filter down the mountain that Uncle Nick still roamed his land.

Two years after Nick's burial, locals made the chimney-shaped marker using granite from the mountain and embedding some of the old man's possessions, such as pots and pans, in the formation. His home was dismantled for the wood and tin it contained, but its imprint still marks the ground by the gravesite. The lyrical poem that embodies Nick's life was apparently written by the man from whom he bought his semi-annual provisions. The shopkeeper of the general store penned the epitaph in honor of a man with a colorful life that was ultimately quite private and full of pain.

The burial site is now maintained by the Appalachian Trail Conference, and many hikers come to this remote site specifically to visit Uncle Nick's grave. But when they stay overnight, they discover that this place contains more than moss-covered turf—there are signs that both Uncle Nick and his trusty hound still patrol their patch of earth. Some nights hikers have heard a spectral dog barking within what sounds like a few feet of their tent, but no animal can be found. They also report hearing a mumbling voice when no one else is seen in the area.

After 40 years of living alone, is it possible that Uncle Nick Grindstaff was ready for some human company? And does Panter still protect his master's territory even though both dog and owner no longer live on this plane? It may be worth an overnight stay to find out.

Cries of the Dead near Cowee Tunnel

Dillsboro, North Carolina

The Cowee Tunnel is 836 feet of hand-carved darkness—a narrow, curving channel that cuts through the formidable mountains west of Dillsboro, North Carolina. It opened up the wilderness and allowed passage by rail through the hills, but the making of the tunnel came at considerable expense. Nineteen men perished in a horrible accident during its construction, and their bodies are buried on a hilltop above the tunnel's southern entrance. Their spirits refuse to let people passing through forget the tragedy that claimed their lives.

In the 1880s, the land-locked residents of western North Carolina wanted to connect up with the "outside world," but that meant finding a path either around or through the mountains for rail travel to move people and goods out of and into the region. For years, the sounds of digging and blasting echoed through the valleys as the Western North Carolina Railroad built the network of lines to link cities such as Asheville and Murphy.

The Cowee Tunnel is on the route between Dillsboro and Bryson City. Built under the guidance of self-educated engineer Captain J.W. Wilson, it was needed to overcome the problem of getting around a nasty hairpin turn in the Tuckasegee River. One of the big obstacles Wilson had to overcome to build the tunnel was the terrain—steep grades, gaping ravines and solid rock. The other challenge was finding enough men willing to risk life and limb for the project. The state solved that one: North Carolina supplied convicts to do the hard labor.

Camp for the convicts happened to be across the roaring waters of the Tuckasegee River, so each day a raft carried the laborers to and from the worksite. Groups of 20 prisoners wore heavy ankle irons and were shackled together to prevent any attempt at escape. On December 30, 1883, those shackles also prevented the men's survival.

In the early morning hours of a frosty winter day, guard Fleet Foster loaded his charge of 20 men onto a ramshackle ferry to begin the trip across the river. As they made their way across the fast-moving water, the rear-end of the ferry began to take on water. Panic ensued and the men rushed aft, causing the boat to capsize. All the men, including Foster, fell into the freezing river. The 19 men chained together sank to the bottom and died. One prisoner, Anderson Drake, had not been in the shackled group and swam to shore. When he realized that Fleet Foster still struggled in the river, Drake went back and rescued the drowning guard.

In a sad twist—and a bit of a digression—Drake did not come out of the story a hero. He was caught stealing Foster's wallet, so instead of receiving a pardon he got lashes and a quick trip back to the tunnel for more hard labor.

A few days after the accident, the bodies of the 19 dead men were recovered and buried in unmarked graves near the mouth of the tunnel. No wonder the screams of shackled prisoners echo so clearly through the eerie passageway. Water dripping from the top of the tunnel's arch is said to be tears of the dead men.

The rough-hewn rocky corridor just looks like a tunnel that would harbor ghosts. As the train passes through murky darkness, with very little clearance, you can practically see the ridges painstakingly carved by human hands. A post on YouTube by someone who traveled the length of the Cowee Tunnel has the following to say about it: "Very haunted, halfway through the tunnel you start getting the chills!!!"

People who have been hiking in the area at night claim to hear clanking and moans coming from inside the tunnel. There have also been reports of feeling like someone— perhaps 19 pairs of spectral eyes?—is watching you.

The rail line is now owned by the Great Smoky Mountain Railroad, and as of August 2008 the railroad stopped running Tuckasegee River excursions (part of which goes through this tunnel) because they shut down the Dillsboro Depot. For those of you who want to experience the tunnel, the staff suggests checking the company website for updated schedules, or call Great Smoky Mountain Railroad offices directly.

The Appalachian Caverns and the Linville Cabin

Blountville, Tennessee

Up on Cave Hill Road in Blountville, Tennessee, are the wondrous Appalachian Caverns. These natural underground caves have housed humans since the seventh century, and it may be that ghosts have been haunting them for almost as long. Archaeological research pinpoints Native American use of the caverns at 675 AD through carbon dating of pottery and arrowheads found deep within the stalactite-filled enclave. But the caves have been in almost continuous use through history, serving as shelter for early pioneering families like the Crockets and the Boones, as a source of vital bat dung to make gunpowder during the American Revolution and the Civil War, and as a hidden moonshine distillery, with the cavern's extensive waterways being used to float the booze to the outer stream. And over time, with so many people bringing their energy to this spot, it also became a place known for its paranormal spirits.

The Native Americans held many spiritual ceremonies within the protective shelter of the caves. The Linville brothers were among the first white men to live in the area; one of them died and is believed to be buried inside somewhere. During the wars the caverns were used as a hospital for soldiers, and certainly many of those men died within the crystal-covered walls. People report hearing male voices echoing through the chambers, and one tourist scurried out in near panic after hearing a blood-curdling scream come from a dark area nearby.

At what is now the commercial entrance to the site stands an old cabin built in 1777. It too is haunted. A chandelier inside the cabin moves of its own accord, and there are reports of seeing the apparition of a small boy wearing old-fashioned clothing who plays with marbles on the floor.

A team of paranormal researchers investigated the caverns in June 2007 and were surprised to see a white orb that was visible to the naked eye. Usually light anomalies are seen only in photographs—and even then are suspect as possible dust specks. This, however, was a "glowing sphere of white light" moving around one of the cavern's rock formations. Other orbs were also seen using some of the team's equipment, and there was a general sense of excitement at witnessing so many light anomalies. Impressed by the amount of inexplicable activity in the cavern, the group plans to conduct further investigations.

The caverns are now a sanctuary for the endangered gray bat as well as half a dozen other bat species, and visitors can take privately run tours through the mile-long labyrinth that winds through rooms with ceilings as high as 135 feet. But if you venture into the caverns, don't assume that the black shadow that flitted just outside peripheral view is a bat—it may be one of the many ghostly entities that still calls this underground lair home.

Helen's Bridge

Beaucatcher Mountain, North Carolina

Helen, come forth!
Helen, come forth!
Helen, come forth!

Uttering this simple phrase three times is all it takes to beckon the ghost of a distraught mother who hanged herself from a bridge on Beaucatcher Mountain in western North Carolina. At least, that is the gist of this story about Helen's bridge. The details are vague and many people feel they amount to little more than an urban legend, but according to Sarah Harrison of the Asheville Paranormal Society, "The bridge is actively haunted. Nearly everyone who goes there has some sort of experience."

There has been much paranormal activity associated with the bridge, from apparitions to orbs of light that many people believe represent the presence of spirit energy. Helen is supposed to wander the mountain in a long gown, searching for her daughter. There have been reports of her appearing at the side of the road and asking passing motorists if they have seen her daughter. Sarah has been visiting the bridge for more than three years. "I've seen orbs and paranormal mist, but I ave never seen Helen myself," she says. "But a number of my group have seen her. They say she had a hideous looking face framed by long hair and was wearing a long, white dress."

The graceful arched bridge with its quarried stone construction was built in 1909 to provide access to Zealandia Castle on the crest of the mountain, and the castle plays a significant part in this ghost story. New Zealand millionaire John Evans Brown built the stone manse in 1884, modeling it after England's Haddon Hall. Sir Phillip S. Henry, a prominent businessman and international diplomat, bought the castle in 1904, doubled the size of the property with a massive granite addition and then filled it with rare, ancient relics.

So who was Helen? Some locals believe Helen was the wife or mistress of Phillip Henry, and when fire broke out in the castle, their only daughter was burned alive. However, other versions of the story suggest that Helen lived in a shack on the mountain with her daughter and that one night someone broke in and attacked her. In the scuffle, an oil lantern was knocked over, and the small cabin quickly succumbed to the flames with Helen's daughter still inside. Either way, Helen's daughter died. Crushed by the loss of her child, Helen took her own life at the end of a rope tied to the bridge.

Although the bridge now bears the grief-stricken woman's name, no records exist to support her suicide there. "We may never know the truth," says Sarah Harrison. "One thing is true. There was a fire at Zealandia, many years ago, that destroyed a room. I've seen video footage of the L.E.M.U.R. investigation of this room. They picked up an EVP [electronic voice phenomenon] of a little girl."

On August 25, 2003, the Asheville-based L.E.M.U.R. Paranormal Investigations, headed by Joshua Warren, investigated the property, which is now being restored as a Historic National Treasure. In the castle room in which Helen's daughter is said to have died, the team recorded a child's voice saying, "Help me, please." The investigators encountered other paranormal energy throughout the castle. Some of the investigators felt the sensation of being touched by something unseen. In another area their EMF (electro-magnetic field) meters spiked off the scale and made bizarre noises never heard before. As the group wandered through the castle basement, team member Brian Irish captured an orb on video that flies through the screen, flitting toward the camera and then moving quickly away before fading out of sight. Could it be that the spirits of mother and daughter are earthbound, in search of each other without realizing that they exist in such close proximity?

Many people visit the bridge on Halloween night to try to conjure Helen. In the various versions of this legend, one common thread is that you must call three times if you wish her spirit to appear. For those who actually do see Helen, the story goes that they might as well set up camp because their cars will no longer start. "People often have car trouble at the bridge," concurs Sarah Harrison. "I had never had a problem with my car before, but my battery died the morning after I visited the bridge."

Be warned: should you venture up the winding roads of Beaucatcher Mountain in search of a ghost, there is more present than the spirit of Helen. Witnesses have seen a large, black, human-shaped thing in the woods adjacent to the bridge. It comes out and chases them down the mountain. They have described being slapped, hit and scratched. "It is definitely paranormal. I think it is probably a non-human entity," says Sarah. "Years ago people used to go up there for occult practices, séances, etc., and they may have stirred up things." Sarah's advice: if you do visit, be respectful, and do not try to invoke or provoke anything up there.

What Burns So Brightly on Brown Mountain?

Burke County, North Carolina

Paranormal investigator Sarah Harrison's journal entry for Monday, November 7, 2005:

I drove up to the 181 overlook near Morganton. When I got there around 7:30, nothing was happening. I thought, dang, drove all the way from Asheville and it's going to be a no show night. I got my flashlight and looked around the overlook; at one end of the parking lot was a couple having a tryst and at the other end was a guy drinking out of a brown paper bag. Great: sex, booze and a paranormal investigator, what a motley crew. As I walked back to my car, the light show started. I saw red, orange and white balls of light on Brown Mountain. They would start out together, pull apart and tumble around. I watched this show for more than an hour. It was still going on when I left at 9:00. It was a clear night, though clouds started moving in about nine. There was a half moon in the sky, and temperature was 55 degrees.

What was it that Sarah witnessed at the lookout to Brown Mountain? Some people say it is the fires of Cherokee women still searching for their dead husbands after a brutal war. Others say it is a dead woman's spirit haunting her murderous husband and alerting people to the whereabouts of her bones. And still others explain it as nothing more than a mirage. But the lights are nothing if not well documented.

They range from a fiery red to yellow and occasionally a spectral shade of blue. They appear singularly or in groups, and every light show is different. Sometimes they dance or whirl about, colliding and cascading in streaks across the sky, and at other times the globes of color simply bob like buoys on the ocean. The idea that the lights are something of an aurora borealis phenomenon has been ruled out, but no other scientific explanation exists, which is somewhat surprising given how long they have been dancing over the long, low ridge known as Brown Mountain.

The first documented account of the lights that shine in Burke County, North Carolina, came from one of the earliest explorers to the region, Geraud de Brahm, a German engineer who tramped through in 1771. The engineer postulated that a nitrous vapor caused the nocturnal spectacle. He wrote that the mountain emitted the vapor, which then— somehow—was ignited by the wind. That "scientific" theory was one of the first to be found false.

Cherokee legends connect the lights to a great war in 1200 between the fierce Cherokee and Catawba nations. According to the Cherokee legend, the lights are cast by the spirits of wives and lovers searching the mountainside endlessly for their dead husbands or sweethearts. Frontiersmen of the time supported a different version of the same tale, espousing the theory that the lights were the spirits of the slain Cherokee and Catawba warriors forever doomed to walk the mountainside.

One of the best views of the lights is from the edge of Linville Gorge at Wiseman's View—named after a relative of balladeer Scotty Wiseman, who in 1961 wrote the blue-grass song "Brown Mountain Lights." The lyrics contain a version of yet another legend around the glowing performance in the sky above the mountain:

High, high on the mountain and down in the canyon below,
It shines like the crown of an angel and fades as the mists
  come and go.
Way, way over yonder, night after night until dawn,
A faithful old slave, come back from the grave,
Is searching, searching for his master who's long, long gone.

The folktale in the song is often told by locals. A planter came to the mountain from the lowlands to hunt but became lost and never returned. The man's slave dutifully came to look for him and hiked all over the mountain night after night carrying his lantern. Now all these years later, the spirit of the slave is said to wander in his never-ending search, still carrying the lantern to guide his way.

One other legend involves the death of a woman named Belinda who married a local man. It was 1850 or so, and mountain folk had to be rugged to survive. Belinda became pregnant, but her husband—an abusive man by all accounts—did not welcome the idea of being a father. He had apparently taken up with another woman, and the two lovers schemed together to make a life that did not include Belinda or the baby. One account suggests that she and the baby disappeared the day the child was born and were never seen again. The community suspected the husband but had no proof, even when searchers found Belinda's bloody bonnet snagged in a bush. But one night the lights appeared in the sky, and people concerned about Belinda took them to be a sign. After watching them for many nights, searchers followed the lights and were led to a mound of stones. Underneath the stones lay the bones of an adult and an infant.

One version of the story maintains that the bones were found many years later, past the time of being able to enact justice. But another version, found in Randy Russell and Janet Barnett's Mountain Ghost Stories and Curious Tales of Western North Carolina, suggests that the locals took Belinda and the baby's skulls and held them over her husband's head—it was believed a criminal could not then lie about the crime. The husband refused to speak, knowing he would be compelled to confess, and from that day forward never spoke another word.

Scientists dismiss these stories as pure myth; however, they do not offer anything substantive to replace the stories, even after more than a century of studying the phenomenon. On September 13, 1913, the *Charlotte Daily Observer* printed an account from a fisherman who saw "mysterious lights just above the horizon every night." That report prompted the United States Geological Survey to send an investigator for some answers. After a brief study, D.B. Stewart announced that the lights did indeed exist, but they were the headlights of trains traveling through the valley and nothing more.

Well, such a nice, tidy answer in such a short time. Everyone from the county went about their business, having been assured there was nothing special about their red, circular orbs and not believing a whit of this new theory. The locals were delighted three years later when a flood disproved Stewart by washing out the railroad tracks and bridges.

Although it took years to rebuild the route, the lights continued to blink and blaze as if nothing had happened.

The U.S. Geological Survey returned a few years later, and
this time the theory was more organic: marsh gases. All their
new-fangled instruments pointed to the spontaneous com-
bustion of gas as the source of the lights. Only a few small
problems arise with that theory: there are no marshes on the
mountain; the lights are seen in the sky, not near the ground
where marsh gases would supposedly combust; and there was
no telltale sign of anything being burned.

So it was back to the drawing board, so to speak. Scientists
were able to rule out reasons for the lights. One report from
1940 proved there were no elements in the soil or rocks that
differed from anywhere else in the area, so why was Brown
Mountain a font of luminescence?

Suddenly everyone wanted in on the game of naming the
source of the lights. The Smithsonian Institution suggested
that this was an example of St. Elmo's fire, which is a weather
phenomenon similar to lightning. But the bright blue or
violet glow of St. Elmo's fire does not occur mid-sky; it needs
a conductor such as a mast, spire, aircraft wings or some
other tall, pointed structure. Another scientist suggested that
the glowing balls of light were a mirage created by a strange
atmospheric charge from nearby towns—not bad, except the
sightings of the lights pre-date the use of electricity. Another
idea proposed that the pitchblende ore deposits found in the
ground, which contain radium, may produce the lights, but
radium rays are not visible to the eye.

Sarah Harrison says the prevailing theory is that the
mountain is full of caves with running water, plus quartz and

magnetite, and that the combination somehow creates an electrical current, which in turn creates the orange and red lights. "It's quite interesting to stand there and watch the lights roll around the mountain," says Sarah. "And though I'm a paranormal researcher, I do feel there probably is a science-based explanation for this. I just can't figure out why no one has come up with something."

In the absence of a sound explanation for the eerie entertainment, legends persist. After all, is it so hard to imagine that Belinda still haunts the hill on which she died? Or that Cherokee spirits continue to roam the land that was theirs for centuries?

Certainly the lights exist—why remains an ongoing mystery. The best time to see them is generally in the fall when the air is cool, according to Sarah. So a trip between September and November may be the ticket to witnessing one of the most famous and least understood phenomena in the Appalachians.

The End

SUSAN SMITTEN is an accomplished television producer, editor and news anchor. She was story editor for the second stellar season of the acclaimed series *Cinema Secrets* on the American Movie Classics network. Smitten has produced and story-edited for Discovery Channel and Life Network and has worked as a senior producer with Great North and Television Renaissance. In a recent project, she produced, wrote and directed segments of a new television series called *Medical Profiles* for Discovery Health, including a one-hour special on actress Carrie Fisher and her struggle with bipolar disorder. The charismatic Smitten is still seen periodically in front of the camera as a current affairs program host on television. When not writing for television, she enjoys combining her journalistic training with her personal interest in folklore to craft ghost story collections.

GHOST HOUSE

COLLECT THE ENTIRE SERIES!

Available through your local bookseller, or order direct.
In Canada, call 1-800-661-9017. In the US, call 1-800-518-3541.
www.lonepinepublishing.com